# Early Childhood Studies

**Also available from Bloomsbury**

Anti-Discriminatory Practice, Rosalind Millam

*Children as Decision Makers in Education*, edited by Sue Cox, Caroline Dyer, Anna Robinson-Pant and Michele Schweisfurth

*Communication, Language and Literacy*, Nichola Callander and Lindy Nahmad-Williams

*Creative Development*, Ashley Compton, Jane Johnston, Lindy Nahmad-Williams and Kathleen Taylor

Education and Constructions of Childhood, David Blundell

*Engaging Fathers in the Early Years*, edited by Carol Potter and Roger Olley

Good Practice in the Early Years, edited by Janet Kay

*Knowledge and Understanding of the World*, Linda Cooper, Jane Johnston, Emily Rotchell and Richard Woolley

Language, Culture and Identity in the Early Years, Tözün Issa and Alison Hatt

*Maria Montessori*, Marion O'Donnell

*Personal, Social and Emotional Development*, Pat Broadhead, Jane Johnston, Caroline Tobbell and Richard Woolley

*Physical Development*, Linda Cooper and Jonathan Doherty

*Problem Solving, Reasoning and Numeracy*, Pat Beckley, Ashley Compton, Jane Johnston and Harriet Marland

Professionalism in the Interdisciplinary Early Years Team, edited by Avril Brock and Carolynn Rankin

Respecting Childhood, Tim Loreman

*Supporting Development in the Early Years Series*, edited by Jane Johnston and Lindy Nahmad-Williams

*Whose Childhood Is It?*, edited by Richard Eke, Helen Butcher and Mandy Lee

**New Childhoods Series, edited by Phil Jones**

Rethinking Children and Families, Nick Frost

Rethinking Children and Research, Mary Kellett

Rethinking Children, Violence and Safeguarding, Lorraine Radford

Rethinking Children's Rights, Sue Welch and Phil Jones

*Rethinking Children's Play*, Fraser Brown and Michael Patte

Rethinking Gender and Sexuality in Childhood, Emily W. Kane

# Early Childhood Studies

## Studies

## A Social Science Perspective

### Ewan Ingleby

BLOOMSBURY

LONDON • NEW DELHI • NEW YORK • SYDNEY

**Bloomsbury Academic**
An imprint of Bloomsbury Publishing Plc

| | |
|---|---|
| 50 Bedford Square | 175 Fifth Avenue |
| London | New York |
| WC1B 3DP | NY 10010 |
| UK | USA |

**www.bloomsbury.com**

First published 2013

**British Library Cataloguing-in-Publication Data**
A catalogue record for this book is available from the British Library.

ISBN: HB: 978-1-4411-2530-9
     PB: 978-1-4411-5614-3

**Library of Congress Cataloging-in-Publication Data**
A catalog record for this title is available from the Library of Congress.

Typeset by Newgen Imaging Systems Pvt Ltd, Chennai, India
Printed and bound in India

# Contents

# Acknowledgements

Thanks go to colleagues and students at Teesside University, UK, and its partner colleges for their contribution to the debates and discussions that have helped to form this book. The book is based on the teaching, learning and professional development reflections of a number of academic staff who are associated with Teesside University. I am indebted to Geraldine Oliver and Rita Winstone, the programme leaders of the Early Childhood Studies programme at Teesside University. In their graceful way, they have both made me realize that every day is an opportunity for learning. Jane Baxendale, Alison Bishop, Amanda Clarkson, Rose Envy, Karen Gibson, Lesley Hagon, Martin Harmer, Clive Hedges, Sally Neaum, Kelly Ptohopoulos, Donald Simpson, Jo Thornhill, Jonathan Tummons, Irene Walker, Rebecca Walters and Paula Willis have also contributed to the discussions that have led to this content. Thanks also go to Professor John Fulton of Surrey University, UK, and Professor John Davis of All Souls College Oxford, UK, for encouraging perseverance in reconciling studying, research, writing, teaching and administrating.

  As ever I am particularly grateful for the support of my parents and my wife Karen and children Bernadette, Teresa and Michael. Without them tomorrow would always be a much harder day.

*Dr Ewan Ingleby*

# Introduction

This book applies social science subjects, such as psychology, sociology, social policy and research methods, to Early Childhood Studies and addresses key aspects of pedagogy and enhancing learning with children under 8. These subjects make an especially important contribution to understanding children's growth and development and applying the social sciences to Early Childhood Studies can help to raise standards and ensure good practice. Clark and Waller (2007, p. 168) draw attention to the 'persistent division' between care and education and the need for strategies to coordinate these services. Doyle (2005, p. 13) comments that this situation can lead to the loss of centrality of the rights of the child especially when the emphasis is placed upon 'policy and procedure' at the expense of recognizing children's needs.

My own realization of the importance of the social sciences to Early Childhood Studies with its explanations of complex aspects of children's behaviour and development occurred when working with children with mental health needs and learning disabilities within residential social work. I had previously studied academic social science and enjoyed interpreting aspects of my own personality and circumstances in relation to psychological and sociological theories. This interest was put into perspective upon experiencing the ways in which children's behaviour can be influenced through the application of psychological therapies. On reflection, the experience of care planning through applying psychological and sociological therapies to particular children was one of the most satisfying aspects of working with children and families. It is a memory that will always stay with me.

One of the key aims of this book is to highlight the ways in which applying the social sciences to Early Childhood Studies increase the effectiveness of professional practice. This application to practice can become a means whereby a balance is offered between what is intrapersonal and particular to individual practitioners alongside what is interpersonal and accepted as being general good practice between practitioners.

# Book structure

This book focuses on six main themes, one within each chapter. Chapter 1 explores some of the key psychological perspectives that are important for Early Childhood Studies. There is an overview of behaviourism, humanism, psychodynamic, cognitive and biological perspectives in relation to a range of professional roles and contexts. In addition to identifying the key ideas of each of the perspectives, we analyse the strengths and weaknesses of each of the perspectives and provide a critical appraisal of the effectiveness of the therapies that have their basis in each of the perspectives. Chapter 2 considers the importance of sociology for Early Childhood Studies within the context of the Childcare Act 2006, which McGillivray (2007, p. 41) acknowledges as legislating for local authorities to work together to meet the needs of children and families. The chapter explores the debate existing between perspectives such as functionalism and interactionism in relation to their lesser or greater acknowledgement of the importance of 'society'. The chapter applies the ideas of these perspectives in accounting for positive and negative social characteristics.

Chapter 3 focuses upon recent initiatives within social policy that have placed children's rights at the centre of statutory legislation. The chapter discusses how and why particular policy directions have been formed and evolved, with discussion of the impact of contemporary policy initiatives for children, families and practitioners.

Chapters 4 and 5 discuss the importance of pedagogy and enhancing learning, exploring children's language acquisition in relation to the development of learning and the need to enhance child development through reflective practice. These chapters use case studies to explore particular aspects of development, such as sensory impairments, learning disabilities and language development deficits. The chapters develop the theme that effective professional practice necessitates being aware of the variety of experiences that help to shape children over time and space.

Chapter 6 takes heed of Handley's warning of 'seeing children as objects of processes rather than subjects' (2005, p. 5) and identifies the key research perspectives and methods that are used within Early Childhood Studies to support the development of professional practice. The chapter begins by identifying the research process before discussing the origins of key research paradigms. The chapter considers key methodological strategies employed by qualitative and quantitative research and concludes with a discussion of the relative merits of research paradigms and methods.

# Learning features

The book attempts to stimulate learning through interactive activities within each chapter. In addition to these activities there are case studies and research tasks. The book aims to support readers to develop analytical skills through a creative engagement with the content. Alongside the interactive learning activities there are supporting references so that knowledge of social science in relation to Early Childhood Studies can be synthesized in relation to these texts.

# Professional development and reflective practice

This book attempts nurture readers who are able to reflect on aspects of best practice to support development in relation to meeting the complex needs of children and families.

# 1 Psychology and Early Childhood Studies

## Learning outcomes

After reading this chapter you should be able to:

- identify what the term psychology means;
- analyse some of the ways that psychology can be used by early years practitioners;
- critically appraise some of the ways that psychology can be applied to early years.

This chapter develops your knowledge and understanding of selected psychological theories accounting for children's growth and development. The material in the chapter explores the idea that an increased awareness of applied psychology enables children to achieve their full potential.

# Introduction

This opening chapter of the book introduces you to the discipline of psychology and discusses how psychology can be applied to early years in order to improve practice. Each school of psychology has a different understanding of what constitutes the self. This understanding is outlined, analysed and critically appraised in order to explore how psychology can be applied to the early years. Throughout the chapter there are formative activities that reinforce learning in relation to the main psychological models that are of relevance for early years practitioners.

# Defining the discipline of psychology

## Reflective Activity 1.1

What is your understanding of the word psychology?

### Feedback

Psychology is an academic discipline that studies a vast range of human and animal behaviour. Psychologists are not mind readers and they do not necessarily have access to our thoughts. They do not work solely with people who are mentally ill or people who are emotionally disturbed. These are common delusions and misinterpretations of the discipline.

'Psychology' is not as easy to define as it might initially appear. It is more than just a word. To a layperson an immediate reaction may be to associate psychology with 'reading peoples' minds' or 'analysing aspects of human behaviour'. A dictionary definition of psychology may give a precise explanation but this precision can disguise the complexity of the subject. An example of a dictionary definition is that psychology can be understood as being:

the scientific study of all forms of human and animal behaviour.

(Online Dictionary)

Psychology is relevant for early years practitioners because it gives explanations for children's growth and development. This means that studying psychology enables you to increase your knowledge of key factors influencing children and families. Practitioners working with children and families may be able to increase their awareness of what influences the developing child and family life by considering the theories that have been generated by the discipline of psychology.

# Origins of psychology

The word psychology is derived from two Greek words 'psyche', meaning mind and 'logos', meaning study so a literal translation of the discipline is 'the study of the mind'. This means that psychology literally translates as the study of the mind. Malim and Birch (1998, p. 3) claim that the academic study of psychology began in 1879 when Wilhelm Wundt opened the first psychology laboratory at the University of Leipzig in Germany. Wundt focused upon 'introspection', meaning observing and analysing the structure of conscious mental processes. It was the emphasis placed upon measurement and control of thinking processes that marked the separation of psychology from its parent discipline philosophy.

## The rise of behaviourism

Malim and Birch (1998, p. 8) argue that by 1920 the usefulness of this method was questioned. John B. Watson was one of a number of theorists who believed that it was wrong to focus upon introspection because this approach to studying psychology is immeasurable and so it invalidated its scientific credentials. Consequently Watson dedicated himself to the study of what has become known as 'behaviourism', or human behaviour that is measurable and observable. Behaviourism remained the dominant force in psychology over the next 30 years, especially in the United States. The emphasis was placed upon identifying the external factors that produce changes in behaviour, learning or conditioning using a stimuli response model.

## Competing perspectives

As with many philosophical and sociological perspectives, psychology is characterized by competing paradigms or models of thought, with theorists becoming grouped together according to which perspective they adopt. Malim and Birch (1998, p. 9) argue that an interesting reaction to behaviourism came in the form of the Gestalt school of psychology emerging in Austria and Germany in the 1920s popularized by psychologists such as Wolfgang Kohler (1927). This branch of psychology takes a holistic approach considering that the person is in totality greater and more complex than his or her individual characteristics. This in turn complicates a focus upon the external factors producing thoughts and behaviour.

## Psychodynamic psychology

A further criticism of behaviourism developed through the twentieth century as a result of the legacy of Sigmund Freud, possibly the most famous psychologist of all. Malim and Birch (1998, p. 9) argue that Freud proposes that the mind is a combination of conscious and unconscious thoughts. If we accept that this is the case, Freud's theory can be used to challenge behaviourism because it implies that human thought and behaviour is more complex than the behaviourist notion that external variables cause thought and behaviour.

## Cognitive psychology

Alongside psychodynamic theory there emerged a further significant theory that places the emphasis upon thinking processes or cognition, in other words the ways in which we attain, retain and regain information. Within cognitive psychology an emphasis is placed on identifying what happens within the mind after a stimulus has been received. The mind is seen as being like an information processor, almost akin to a computer. Malim and Birch (1998, p. 25) explain this perspective by arguing that 'human beings are seen as information processors who absorb information from the outside world, code and interpret it, store and retrieve it'. In a literal revolution of thought, thinking has come back full-circle and the initial criticism of introspection being unlikely to explain the complexity of human thought is asserted within this psychological theory.

## Biological psychology

This view is reinforced by some of the current developments within psychology. The scientific advances of the 1990s and beyond in relation to identifying the genetic and hormonal composition of the human mind have generated enormous interest in the idea that thoughts and behaviour are determined by our biology. This may be considered to be a reductionist argument because it reduces complex thoughts and behaviour to a few variables such as hormones and genes. The ideas within biological psychology may prove to be yet another passing paradigm contributing to the on-going dialogue about the discipline of psychology that in turn will be criticized and revised.

From this initial discussion about what is meant by the word psychology we can ask a further question in relation to the nature of the human mind. 'Is the human mind the same as the human brain?'

---

### Reflective Activity 1.2

Do you think that the mind is the same as the brain? List three reasons why the mind might be regarded as being the same as the brain. Why might a different argument be developed that essentially argues that the mind is different to the brain?

### Feedback

One answer to this question is that there is no definite answer. Philosophers have speculated for hundreds, perhaps thousands, of years about what has come to be known as 'the mind-brain problem'. Whether you focus upon the mind or the brain depends upon your fundamental understanding of how psychology should be studied. Many psychological perspectives such as behaviourism, humanism, psychodynamic and cognitive theories emphasize the importance of the mind. This is because each of these perspectives has a clear understanding or model of the mind. In contrast biological perspectives are more likely to place an emphasis upon the genes and hormones influencing the brain.

We can now look at exploring some of the psychological perspectives. This is a way of adding detail to our introductory explanations of what the subject area of psychology is. It is also a means of setting the scene before we look at how psychology can be applied to early years practice and Early Childhood Studies in particular.

---

# The schools of psychology

Table 1.1 gives a summary of five major schools of psychology together with a brief description of their key features.

These schools of thought are especially useful to practitioners working with children and families because of the influence they have had in shaping the academic concerns of psychology. The practical application of this academic discipline appears to relate to much of the work that is undertaken with children and families. If you are working with children and families you will need to apply psychology through 'modelling' best practice and meeting the needs of children and families in an assertive manner. Knowledge and understanding of the competing perspectives in psychology can help you to achieve this 'best practice'. The origins of the schools of thought go back to some of the earliest philosophical ideas to have influenced Western

**Table 1.1** Schools of psychology

| School | Key features |
| --- | --- |
| Behaviourism | Human behaviour is seen as being shaped by environmental forces and is a collection of learned responses to external stimuli. The key learning process is known as 'conditioning'. |
| Humanism | The individual is seen as being unique, rational and self-determining. Present experience is held to be as important as past experience. |
| Psychodynamic theory | The mind is seen as being a combination of conscious thoughts and the workings of the unconscious mind. The unconscious mind expresses itself through dreams and behaviour we are not consciously aware of. |
| Cognitive theory | This perspective looks at what happens after a stimulus but before a response. The human mind is likened to a computer. People are seen as information processors, selecting, coding, storing and retrieving information when needed. |
| Neurobiological theory | Behaviour is considered as being determined by genetic, physiological and neurobiological factors and processes. |

thought. The proposition that there are forces beyond the individual that shape social reality goes back to the ideas of the Greek philosopher Plato. This idea is central to behaviourism so the perspective has its intellectual origins in this classical thought. The notion that individuals interpret their social world as opposed to being ultimately shaped by this world goes back to the ideas of Aristotle (Audi, 1995). This philosophy is of central importance to humanism. In other words the genesis of the perspective's dominant idea can be traced back to these early times. A summary of each of the key perspectives developing the definitions given in Table 1.1 follows. A definition of each of the key perspectives is given, key figures influencing the perspective are identified and central terms within each perspective are explained.

# Behaviourism

Behaviourists emphasize the importance of external factors in producing thoughts within the human mind. A key behaviourist idea is that every individual enters the world as a 'clean slate'. The surrounding environment is considered to be the 'chalk' etching its marks upon the 'slate' of the mind. This means that the individual enters the world without a fixed identity and that social factors are responsible for making the individual whosoever she/

he becomes. The Jesuit notion of 'giving me the boy and I'll show you the man' equates to this idea. This suggests that we become who we are as a result of factors beyond and outside individuals.

A number of psychologists have become famous members of the behaviourist school of thought. Burrhus Skinner, Edward Thorndike, John Watson and Ivan Pavlov have become synonymous with behaviourist psychology. All of these psychologists share in common the belief that external factors are of critical importance in producing thoughts and behaviour.

The terms 'classical conditioning' and 'operant conditioning' are particularly important within behaviourism. Classical conditioning is associated with the work of Ivan Pavlov. It has become associated with the ways whereby biological responses are regulated by external factors. This produces what has become phrased as a 'conditioned response' where a form of behaviour occurs in association with a particular stimulus. Operant conditioning is a term that has become associated with the work of Burrhus Skinner. It refers to the link that exists between positively affirming behaviour that reinforces a particular stimulus. To give a simple example, if a child responds favourably to a parental instruction the child is usually praised. This reinforcement of learning through praise is therefore a type of operant conditioning. In the following case study there is the exemplification of when children may experience classical and operant conditioning.

## Case study

Sophie is 4 years old and she has just started school. She has been in the school for 1 month and she has already learned many of the school rules. She has noticed that when the school bell rings at 9 a.m. she has to line-up with all the other children and stand still with her arms by her side looking out for her class teacher Mrs Black. At first a number of the infants did not know what to do when the bell rang at the start of the school day. The sight of all the other children moving into line upset some of the infants as they felt afraid and anxious because they did not know what they were supposed to do. This association of the bell ringing and anxiety has gradually made the infants copy what the other older children do. Today when the bell rang at 9 a.m. nearly all of the infants copied the other older children so that they would not stand out and feel anxious. They got into line standing with their arms by their sides looking out for Mrs Black. They moved a little bit more than the other older children but their response to the bell ringing at 9 a.m. has become conditioned into acceptable behaviour. On Friday Sophie received a 'star badge' for her good work. She felt very pleased as she had to go onto the stage at assembly and receive her gold badge. Sophie remembered her parents' words that in school she should always try her hardest.

---

### Reflective Activity 1.3

What would interest behaviourist psychologists about Sophie?

### Feedback

Behaviourist psychology is associated with classical and operant conditioning. A simple understanding of these two types of conditioning is that whereas classical conditioning is interested in how biological reactions are influenced by external factors, operant conditioning is concerned with how choices are influenced by external factors. The case study is relevant to both types of conditioning. The 'fear' and 'anxiety' produced by the external environment (or school) is a physical response that is generated by an external factor. The 'learned response' by Sophie to 'try her hardest' is an example of operant conditioning.

---

# Humanism

Humanism does acknowledge the importance of environmental factors on the mind but it places an emphasis upon the individual interpretation of external factors. This means that as opposed to emphasizing the importance of external variables, attention is given to the importance of individuals interpreting social reality. Humanism can be associated with the philosophy of Immanuel Kant and his 'Copernican revolution' of thought (Audi, 1995, p. 400). As opposed to asking about the reality of the universe, Kant changes the focus of the argument to ask about how individuals understand social reality. Humanism asks a similar question. As opposed to focusing upon how external variables produce thoughts, the humanist emphasis is on how individuals make sense of external variables.

Humanism has become associated with the work of Carl Rogers and Abraham Maslow. Maslow proposes that all humans have a 'hierarchy of needs' and that individual thoughts are influenced by the extent to which these physiological and intellectual needs are being met. Carl Rogers has had a particularly important influence on humanism and it may be claimed that

Rogers is the founding father of psychological humanism. His work is also influential in what is considered as being effective early years practice. One of the most important Rogerian ideas to have influenced social care is the proposal that anxiety is a product of what has become termed as a 'would/should dilemma'. This means that an individual wants to do something but they are unable to achieve this wish. According to Rogers this then generates tension within the individual that in turn produces anxiety.

In applying therapy to resolve the would/should dilemma, Rogers recommends that the therapist must have a 'congruent' or genuine interest in the person. This means that empathy is a central concept to the Rogerian model of client-centred therapy. The ideal aim is to lead the person being counselled to their 'inner beautiful self' so that the individual's would/should dilemma can be overcome.

## Reflective Activity 1.4

Think about your own personal development. To what extent do you think that your personality has been formed as a result of external environmental factors? To what extent do you think that your personality is a product of your unique personality?

### Feedback

Most people would probably accept that their personality is a combination of external environmental variables alongside their own unique personal traits. In other words the person is a product of factors that are both outside and inside the individual. It is interesting, however, to consider why and when the emphasis placed upon the individual and the environment varies. In this country particular social, economic and religious variables have influenced the extent to which one's surroundings or one's personality are held accountable for personality development. In the United Kingdom there are many communities that emphasize self-responsibility. If one claims that the environment is responsible for personal development this may be regarded as an attempt to disown one's accountability for individual life circumstances. Some of the popular movements of the 1960s and 1970s may have changed this perception but the prevailing thought in the United Kingdom today would seem to be that individual characteristics are especially important in determining one's personality. This may lessen the importance of the behaviourist perspective and make humanism a more influential explanation of individual circumstances.

# Psychodynamic theory

Psychodynamic psychology is associated with the ideas of one of the most famous psychologists, Sigmund Freud. Freud's theory postulates that thoughts are a product of the working of both the conscious and the unconscious mind (Gross, 2001, p. 969). We have conscious thoughts that we are aware of and unconscious thoughts that appear in our mind in the form of dreams. Moreover, what happens in our conscious mind in turn influences what thoughts filter through to our unconscious mind.

Freud considers that there are three especially important components to every individual (Gross, 2001, p. 591). There is the 'id' or biological physiology of maleness and femaleness. There is the 'ego' or social self to regulate our biological 'id'. There is also the 'superego' existing beyond the individual that generates a common understanding of our social identity.

Freud claims that all individuals go through a number of stages of development. From 0 to 1 a child is considered to be in an oral stage of development. This means that the infant is preoccupied with its mouth. This then leads to the anal stage of development from 1 to 2 when the infant becomes aware of its capacity to excrete and urinate. The next developmental stage is the phallic stage of development when boys and girls become increasingly aware of biological maleness and femaleness. Freud claims that this occurs between the ages of 3–6 resulting in a close relationship between a boy and his mother and a girl and her father. After the phallic stage of development there is what Freud terms as a latent phase of development. This occurs between the ages of 6–12 as the individual becomes more concerned with their social identity as they become increasingly aware of their ego state. The theory states that the final stage of development is the genital stage from the age of 12 onwards when Freud proposes that males and females become increasingly aware of their adult reproductive capabilities.

Freud's theory introduces the idea that human beings hold the potential for fixated behaviour. This means that an individual could become negatively confined to a particular stage (or stages) of development. As an example, if an infant experienced the trauma of losing its mother at the age of 1, there is the possibility of this individual developing what Freud terms an 'oral fixation'. This fixated behaviour expresses itself at a later age through consciously chosen behaviour exemplified by the oral fixation of alcoholism. What makes the theory so original is that it is claimed that the conscious choice of behaviour has its origins in the repressed depths of the unconscious mind. Proponents of the theory claim that this repression can be released through psychodynamic counselling. This counselling may be needed in a situation when the individual has experienced a physical and/or emotional crisis during their development.

Crises leading to fixated behaviour can occur at any stage of development. According to Freud this personal development directs the individual in the direction of one of two forces, either towards 'Thanatos' or 'Eros'. Eros, the Greek god of love is interpreted by Freudians as contributing to an individual's optimism. Thanatos, the Greek personification of death is perceived as contributing to an individual's sense of pessimism. How one develops determines whether one's conscious frame of mind directs the individual to the good or otherwise. It can be argued that Freud's legacy is to have left one of the most influential psychological theories to contribute to the discipline. It is however important to recognize that just because the theory is famous does not mean it is correct. This point will be developed later in the chapter.

# Cognitive theory

Cognitive psychology can be understood as being a branch of psychology that is interested in what happens after a stimulus but before a response. It is a school of psychology that has become associated with the work of Jean Piaget and Lev Vygotsky. Malim and Birch (1998, p. 27) argue that Piaget is 'the most significant figure in the study of cognitive development'. Piaget's model of cognitive development has become particularly influential within psychology. According to Piaget the human mind develops over time as an individual is stimulated by its surroundings. From the ages of 0–2 the child has basic thoughts or 'schemata'. Piaget claims that these initial thoughts are limited and instinctive. A baby has a 'crying schema', a 'grasping schema' and a 'feeding schema'. These thought processes develop from the age of 2 as the infant becomes capable of speech and develops what Piaget phrases as 'symbolic thought'. It is also proposed that between the ages of 2–7 the child's problem-solving skills are limited because of two terms Piaget phrases as 'centration' and 'egocentricism'. By 'centration' Piaget means that the child can see one aspect of a situation's reality but not the total picture. As an example, a child between the ages of 2–7 may think that a tonne of lead is heavier than a tonne of feathers because they 'centrate' or focus on one aspect of the problem. The child assumes that lead is a metal and therefore heavier than 'fluffy' feathers. This means that the child may not see that in fact both quantities are the same weight. By 'egocentrism' Piaget means that a child cannot see the true nature of a problem because problem solving occurs in relation to what the child knows about reality. As an example, if a child aged 2–7 is asked what noise a reindeer makes they may say 'clip clop' instead of 'I don't know'. This is due to egocentrism. The child thinks that the reindeer looks like a horse and knows that a horse makes a 'clip clop' sound so it assumes that reindeer also makes a 'clip clop' sound. Piaget claims that in order to progress through this stage of development the child needs to interact with its environment through play.

As a consequence of linguistic development the infant becomes capable of more complex thought so that by the age of 7 the preoperational stage has ended and the child is able to complete complex problem solving. This stage of development is phrased 'concrete operations'. This is because Piaget claims that children aged between 7 and 11 need to use props if they are to complete problem-solving activities. From 7 to 11 a child can calculate that 3 apples + 2 apples add up to make 5 apples but Piaget claims that the child needs to have the actual apples at hand in order to complete the calculation. As this interaction occurs the child will develop what Piaget phrases as 'reversible thinking'. This is the final stage of cognitive development occurring around 11 years of age. Once reversible thought has been reached it is possible to 'problem solve' within the mind, without using the props that a 7-year-old child needs. When one can apply reversible thinking to solving a problem, it means that one can see within one's mind that 3+2 is the same as 7–2.

Lev Vygotsky's work is seen as complementing Piaget's theory as opposed to being a radically different cognitive perspective (Malim and Birch, 1998, p. 469). Vygotsky places more emphasis upon the social factors influencing the child's cognitive development. One of Vygotsky's central ideas is the notion of each individual having a 'scaffold' of persons aiding their cognitive development. According to the nature of the scaffold, the child's cognitive development is affected in either negative or positive ways. If for example the child's peers are interested in academic issues, this social scaffold will impact upon cognitive development and make the child more academic. If the opposite situation occurs it leads to negative cognitive development. It can be argued that this theory complements Piaget's work because it explains why some children are 'late developers' and reach the stage of reversible thought beyond the age of 11. Vygotsky uses the term 'ZPD' or

'Zone of Proximal Development' to refer to when an individual has fulfilled their cognitive potential. This stage of development may occur at 11. It may occur beyond the age of 11. What becomes critical is the influence of one's cognitive development in relation to the 'scaffold' of individuals influencing one's cognitive development.

# Biological psychology

It can be argued that biological psychology is becoming of increasing importance due to the recent scientific advances in particular in relation to understanding human genetics. The biological perspective places an emphasis on the link between the thoughts of individuals and their hormonal and chromosomal composition. It is accepted by the scientific community that males and females differ in one pair of chromosomes and that before the infant is born the presence of a 'Y' chromosome leads to the development of testes. This in turn leads to the production of the hormone testosterone. As a consequence males produce more androgens whereas females produce oestrogen and progesterone. Biologists such as Milton Diamond (1980) and Roger Gorski et al. (1966) have been responsible for this school of psychology gathering academic momentum. The key idea considers the importance of biology in producing thoughts. It has been discovered that the male brain is physically different to the female brain due to the influence of the hormone testosterone. According to this theory the inevitable consequence is that the thoughts occurring within the mind must have some biological basis and that differences in thought patterns are crucially linked to hormonal and chromosomal factors.

# Applying psychology to early years

All of the psychological perspectives that have been introduced within this chapter can be applied to early years practice and to Early Childhood Studies. There are a number of psychological therapies and each one has the potential to improve and enhance professional practice. Moreover if the therapies are combined they offer the potential to give holistic therapy in order to assist children with complex needs. This section of the chapter introduces some of the therapies that could be used by practitioners working with children and families. This is one example of how psychology can be applied to the early years context.

## Behaviourist therapies

One of the most well-known behaviourist therapies is called 'token economy'. The therapy is based on the principle of conditioning responses, effectively manipulating choice so that positive behaviour occurs. Most children have complex thoughts and they are likely to choose whether to conform with or rebel against accepted social requirements. This acceptance or rebellion can be overt and explicit or implicit and assumed. Token economy attempts to produce conformity of response. At the end of every day in which the individual has complied with what is required a reward or 'token' is offered. This token has to have appeal and value to the person receiving the therapy. If there is a lack of compliance with the programme the token is denied. After a short period of time, for example 5 days of compliance, the recipient is rewarded with a bigger treat or prize. Token economy is used within many nurseries and primary schools. It is a behaviourist attempt to get children to comply with what is required of them within the school environment. It is a therapy that is also used within other early years contexts, but as we shall see later in the chapter, it is a therapy that is not without its critics.

Another therapy that is available for early years practitioners is biofeedback. This therapy may be used with children who have been referred for professional help because they are highly anxious. Music, light, aroma and relaxing furnishings are combined to produce an environment that can physically relax the individual. The therapy is essentially attempting to produce relaxing thoughts within the child's mind by manipulating external variables.

A third popular therapy that has its origins within behaviourist theory is known as 'systematic desensitization'. This therapy may be used with children who have phobias. The child is made to come to terms with his/her phobia in a controlled environment. It is proposed that as a result of gradually exposing the child to the phobia in a non-threatening way, the phobic object becomes manageable and increasingly less debilitating. Once again the emphasis is placed upon the importance of the practitioner manipulating the child's thoughts in order to produce positive ways of thinking about the phobia. The following case study example outlines the ways in which behaviourism can be applied to early years. It also reveals some of the potential difficulties that exist when particular therapies are applied to children with particular needs.

## Case study

Peter lives in residential care. He is 7 and has learning disabilities but there has been no definitive diagnosis of the nature of his disability. He is thought to have a combination of autism and learning disability. Before Peter goes to sleep at night he has a habit of getting all of his shoes from his wardrobe and throwing them down the stairs. In an attempt to get Peter to change his behaviour a token economy programme has been designed by the members of the multidisciplinary team who work with him. Peter loves watching cartoons on television and the token economy programme involves giving Peter a token on each day when he does not throw his shoes down the stairs. Peter likes chocolate and when he has complied with the care programme he is given a chocolate treat of his choice. If he does not follow what is expected of him Peter is denied this reward. Upon receiving five tokens, Peter is given the opportunity to watch a cartoon DVD of his choice. Some of the staff working with Peter have expressed concerns that there are ethical problems with this behaviour modification programme. There are concerns that this conditioning violates Peter's right to choose what he should and should not do.

### Reflective Activity 1.5

If this form of therapy does work and modifies behaviour do you think the therapy should be applied to working with children and families?

### Feedback

You could argue that being an effective practitioner means influencing the lives of children and families. As an example, a teacher needs to be able to motivate students in order to be effective. If, however, influencing the lives of children and families becomes equated with manipulating behaviour in a way that does not respect children and families, this may be seen as being an example of poor professional practice.

# Humanist therapies

The humanist philosophy of Carl Rogers is at the centre of what is deemed as being 'good practice' within early years work. Rogers proposes an egalitarian model of practice in which the practitioner is not aloof from the child but 'with' the child. Empathy is a particularly important aspect of the Rogerian way. The practitioner must be there for the child and prepared to be genuine and assertive. According to Rogers a genuine practitioner can enable children's growth and development.

Effective practice is facilitated upon resolving the 'would/should dilemma'. Rogers considers that this dilemma is the cause of anxiety that in turn prevents child development. Practitioners should also direct children to their 'beautiful inner self'. Rogers believes that all individuals are innately good and that it is only the tension that results from a would/should dilemma that makes the individual a less than good person. Through a genuine and empathetic relationship it is postulated that the would/should dilemma will be replaced by an assertive awareness of one's inner goodness. Although there are many applications for this type of therapy, the generalizing assumptions that are made within humanism can mean that its application is restricted. This argument is exemplified in the following case study example and in the final section of the chapter.

## Case study

Julie has recently qualified as a teaching assistant and she is working with children aged 7–8 in an inner city school. Within the last few months there has been an escalation of racial tension between black and white youths. The situation is further complicated by an outbreak of violence between Asian and Afro-Caribbean youths. As a student Julie was inspired by the ideas of Carl Rogers during a 'Promoting Positive Behaviour' module and she bases her teaching approach upon the principles of client-centred therapy. Within one of her first teaching sessions with a young Asian boy, Julie is devastated when the child runs out of the classroom when she is reading a story to the children. Julie realizes that her values are very different from the values of this child and that this limits the application of client-centred therapy. In the past she has found that this therapy works with White children who seem to share many of her values but it is an altogether different challenge applying these ideas in this particular context.

---

### Reflective Activity 1.6

Do you think that Rogerian therapy is more likely to work with younger or older children?

### Feedback

In the United Kingdom 'early years' is associated with working with children aged from 0 to 8 years of age. Although it is difficult to generalize it may be the case that younger children (who are 8 years and below) are more likely to respond better to Rogerian therapy. As children grow towards adolescence they need to develop their own personality. This may mean that they prefer to develop their own ideas and that they contradict the suggestions of others as this is regarded as 'limiting' their personal development. In contrast, younger children may see adults as being so important that they want to imitate their behaviour in order to 'please'. This may mean that it is easier to apply Rogerian therapy with these younger children.

---

## Psychodynamic therapies

The psychodynamic model of the mind holds that conscious thoughts are influenced by the unconscious mind. This means that therapy involves releasing what is being unconsciously repressed. This then enables the individual to deal with these thoughts within the conscious mind. The psychodynamic therapist is responsible for interpreting what is within the individual's unconscious mind by analysing dreams and/or using hypnotherapy. Dream and fantasy analysis become a means of interpreting what is being repressed. It is considered to be imperative for repressed unconscious thoughts to be released into the conscious mind in order to lessen the effects of repression. The Freudian model holds that fixated behaviour has its basis in repression so that the critical role of the therapist is one of releasing repressed thoughts and then recommending ways of consciously dealing with these thoughts.

The psychodynamic model is hierarchical as opposed to being equalitarian. The omniscient therapist is in a position of power over his/her clients, a characteristic that can be deemed as being opposed to the equalitarian approach of Carl Rogers. This has consequences for the situations in which the therapy can be used and the clients upon whom the therapy should be used. This critique of psychodynamic therapy is exemplified in the subsequent case study.

## Case study

Daniel is 6 and he has not attended school for over 5 months because he suffers from 'panic attacks''. He does not know why he experiences these panic attacks but he says that whenever he thinks about going to school he is unable to eat and that he has 'butterflies' in his stomach. Since there is no conscious explanation for his panic attacks, Daniel's psychiatrist has recommended a number of hypnotherapy sessions in order to identify if there is an unconscious repressed reason for Daniel's behaviour. Under hypnosis Daniel talks about his anxieties about school, in particular his fear of some of the older pupils and of a recent incident when an older boy physically assaulted him in the school yard. Daniel had never disclosed this incident to anyone before and this was thought to be a major benefit of the hypnotherapy sessions. When Daniel was asked about this incident after his hypnotherapy had finished he said that this wasn't the main reason for his fear of school and that he still did not know why he was having his panic attacks. This was a difficulty of the hypnotherapy sessions. Although it did appear to shed light on some of the things that Daniel was repressing it still did not explain a reason for the panic attacks that both Daniel and his psychiatrist could unanimously agree upon. Daniel's psychiatrist said that he thought Daniel was having panic attacks because he was afraid of being bullied but Daniel denied this and said he didn't know what was causing the anxiety.

### Reflective Activity 1.7

Why might psychodynamic therapies be criticized as being a 'mystery'?

### Feedback

The difficulty with psychodynamic therapies appears to be that sometimes they work and other times they do not appear to work. The unconscious mind is a nebulous realm that is not fully understood. As the therapies involve this mysterious part of the mind, this is why the therapies may be associated with uncertainty.

## Cognitive therapies

Cognitive psychologists emphasize the importance of studying what happens after a stimulus but before a reaction. They are interested in the processes within the mind that produce thoughts, not in a biological sense but in terms of cognitive processes. It is proposed that through manipulating these cognitive processes one's thought processes can change. If, for example a child is unable to control their anger, it may be possible to apply cognitive therapy so that this anger is effectively managed. By counselling the individual to consciously change the thought processes occurring within the mind so that they think differently, there follows a cognitive restructuring. This allows the individual to think about the world in a different way. It is a therapy relying on psychological techniques as opposed to a medical therapy. If it is combined with other psychological therapies it can offer a potential solution to various psychological problems such as low self-esteem and inability to manage anger. The following case study example outlines how cognitive therapy can be applied to a particular example of anger management.

## Case study

Taylor is 5 and comes from a travelling family who have recently settled into the local community. He has a younger sister but his father has left the family home. Taylor is becoming prone to increasingly violent outbursts. It appears that he gradually becomes angry and then attacks his mother, his sister or both. Taylor's mother has become very concerned about these outbursts. In a recent incident Taylor screamed at his sister that he was going to 'strangle' her and Taylor's mother admitted that she was finding it hard to cope. The family have been helped by social services and Taylor's social worker referred the child to a cognitive behaviourist therapist who began to counsel Taylor. The therapy seemed to have some success when Taylor and his mother attended the sessions. It was explained to Taylor's mother that she must always maintain control of the situation when Taylor was having these outbursts by thinking in a non-aggressive and assertive way. When Taylor was having an aggressive outburst he had to be isolated from his mother and his sister. Taylor's mother was told that she should go and see Taylor at 5-minute intervals to ask if he had 'calmed down' so that Taylor would learn that a consistent strategy was in place to deal with his violent outbursts. The combination of anger management and applied behaviourism seemed to make a dramatic difference in controlling Taylor's violent outbursts.

**Reflective Activity 1.8**

What do you think is the most effective way for a therapist to manage excessive 'anger' displayed by clients?

**Feedback**

The above case study appears to show that anger is being managed effectively by the therapies being used. It is also interesting to see that it is not just one therapy that is being applied but that cognitive and behaviourist therapies are being combined together. This may help in providing holistic therapy in order to meet the complex challenges that cannot be resolved by just one psychological therapy.

# Biological therapies

Biological psychology attempts to understand the human mind by applying traditional Western scientific principles. Therapies are based on the idea that thought processes are determined by the genetic and hormonal nature of the brain. It is also proposed that thought processes can be influenced by drug therapy. As an example, an overly aggressive child may be diagnosed as being overly aggressive because of the presence of too much testosterone within the body. This male hormone may need to be regulated by medication that lessens the aggressive impulses that are produced within the mind.

In the application of therapies based upon biological psychology, early years workers may be required to monitor the drug therapy of particular children. To give an example, it has been discovered that in some instances placing the individual on a drug regime based on dopamine can regulate schizophrenia. If levels of dopamine within the brain determine the presence or otherwise of schizophrenic tendencies it can be argued that drug therapies have their value within early years practice. It may also be argued that the precise link between the chemical composition of the brain and human thought processes has never been exactly established and that this psychological perspective has not developed as yet to the extent that it can offer every possible solution for every possible psychological need.

**Reflective Activity 1.9**

Think about each of the schools of psychology outlined in Table 1.1 and suggest how they might explain child obesity.

⇨

### Feedback

Each of the psychological schools of thought would answer the question differently. Behaviourist psychologists think that the external environment shapes the individual. This means that obesity is considered to be a form of learned behaviour. The way to change the behaviour is through systems of reward and punishment that encourage healthy eating and discourage 'binge eating'. Humanists such as Carl Rogers would interpret obesity as being a sign of anxiety. Anxiety is a product of what Rogers describes as a 'would/should' dilemma, in other words an individual is not able to do what they would like to do. Resolve this dilemma and they are less likely to become obese. Psychoanalysts consider that conscious thoughts are influenced by what is within the unconscious mind. Obesity is considered to be a conscious fixation resulting from a repressed unconscious experience. It may be postulated that when the individual was a baby they had a traumatic experience during their oral stage of development and that the conscious act of 'binge eating' is a means of releasing this repressed thought. The way to resolve this fixation is to have psychodynamic counselling whereby the counsellor can help the individual to resolve the conflict between unconscious and conscious thoughts. Neurobiological psychologists explain behaviour through analysing an individual's genetic composition. The implication is that obesity is a genetic disorder. The way to stop obese behaviour is to isolate and amend the biological gene promoting this behaviour. At present this procedure is talked about as opposed to being done. Cognitive psychologists would explain obesity as being part of an individual's cognitive map or thinking processes. It is a type of behaviour that comes from within the mind. In order to stop individuals' 'binge eating' it may be proposed that the individual needs to have a cognitive restructuring of their thinking processes via cognitive counselling.

### Practical task

When you are in an early years setting take a research diary and make a note of which therapies are being applied by the staff you meet. Analyse the effectiveness of the therapies by identifying which therapies work and why you think they are working. Make sure that you respect principles of confidentiality!

We can now complete our introductory chapter by focusing our discussion on critically appraising the psychological perspectives in terms of their value for early years.

# Psychological therapies and the early years

There is no single perspective that holds all the answers to solving the problems faced by many children within early years settings. This means that the psychological therapies that have been outlined have limitations if they are applied in isolation.

## Appraising behaviourism

The behaviourist therapies that have been summarized can make the mistake of focusing upon external variables to such an extent that the particular needs of individuals are not met. Every human being does not react in the same way to an external response. Even complex mammals such as dolphins can defy the laws of operant conditioning by doing the opposite to what they are expected to do. This means that there can be no scientific certainty of the therapies that are informed by this perspective. There is a further difficulty with behaviourist therapies that may be summarized as being linked to the unique nature of the human mind. There are profound ethical difficulties with therapies such as token economy. It can be claimed that token economy programmes do not respect dignity and human rights. A token economy programme is essentially saying 'do this for me and you will be rewarded'. This is a power relationship and it could be argued that the child is being manipulated in hierarchical non-egalitarian ways. This means that there are critiques of behaviourist therapies and concerns that they have limited application to early years. It leads Malim and Birch (1998, p. 24) to criticize behaviourist therapies because they can be 'mechanistic' and that they 'overlook the realm of consciousness and subjective experience'.

## Appraising humanism

It can also be proposed that there are limitations in the application of Rogerian client-centred therapy. For the child to accept the importance of resolving the would/should dilemma it is important that they share similar values to the therapist. The child needs to accept that the values of the therapist are important so that there can be a situation where there is a link between what both therapist and client want to achieve. There are, however, many instances when the values of the child may be opposed to the values of the therapist. This can be exemplified within a school environment in which the pupils do not want to achieve what their teachers perceive as being important. This is supported by research that has been completed on the 'chava' subculture within the north-east of England. It is also acknowledged by Anne Watson (2004) in her discussion of the failings of the wider academic curriculum within the United Kingdom. Watson argues that it is not so much that the curriculum is a 'bad idea', it is more that there is little awareness of how to unite the values of the children and their teachers. This can mean that if an early years worker is to attempt using the ideas of Rogers the therapy cannot work because there is no common understanding of what is important and achievable. It is all very well to say that a would/should dilemma should be resolved but a child can only be directed to their 'inner beautiful self' if they perceive that self through a shared sense of identity with their therapist. Malim and Birch (1998, p. 803) develop this criticism by arguing that a critical limitation with humanist therapies relates to the assumption that 'self-actualization' is a principal human motivation. Self-actualization may motivate particular groups of individuals but it cannot be assumed to be a universal characteristic of every human being at every point in time.

## Appraising psychodynamic theory

It may be argued that psychodynamic therapy has as many limitations as uses. The model is not based upon a sound methodology and many of the theoretical ideas can be challenged. It is a theory that is built upon assumptions of how the mind operates. If this is the case, it can be argued that any successes within psychodynamic theory are due to good fortune as much as anything else. A more significant critique of psychodynamic therapy is that it is a theory that is laden with negative value assumptions. The therapist is perceived to be in control of interpreting the child's problems. The classic image of the psychiatric couch can be applied to psychodynamic theory. This means that there is no equality of dialogue. As opposed to influencing the therapeutic process, the individual is effectively disempowered by a therapist who tells 'what should be done' in order to resolve 'fixated behaviour'. Malim and Birch (1998, p. 802) reinforce this criticism by emphasizing that within psychoanalytical therapies there are problems of 'validation'. It may be suggested that within psychodynamic therapy the truth is invented as opposed to being truth in itself.

## Appraising cognitive theory

The cognitive psychology of Jean Piaget can also be criticized. It is a theory that may have been mistranslated and turned into an unworkable model of the mind. Can it be accepted that the human brain moves through the stages that have become accepted as integral to Piaget's model? If not and if thoughts develop through more of a process than the movement through distinct stages of development, it means that the potential application of cognitive therapy is called into question. A further criticism is that although one can take apart a computer and identify the microchips making up its component parts, the human brain is altogether more complex. All sorts of factors that are not necessarily conscious inform cognitive processes. This may mean that a perspective that focuses upon what happens after a stimulus but before a response is dealing with part of the picture, but not the whole picture of human thought. A further criticism of cognitive therapy is that the child's challenging behaviours or thoughts are always changed to those that the therapist sees as being acceptable. Malim and Birch (1998, p. 801) question whether it can always be the case that the therapist has the correct perspective on the world and that the child's cognitive outlook is in need of total change.

## Appraising biological psychology

The biological therapies that are available to early years may be criticized because of what we do not know as opposed to what we do know. There is still much work that needs to be done in order to understand the hormonal and genetic composition of the brain. There is also a degree of uncertainty as to why some chemical treatments work with some individuals and yet the same treatments are less effective in another identical context. This anxiety can be combined with the concern existing over the side effects of drug-based therapy and the ethical implications this has for children. Taking a particular pill might make someone less aggressive but if the consequences are the docility exemplified in *One Flew Over the Cuckoo's Nest* this effectively reduces the individual's life chances. There is also the critique that biological psychology is reductionist. It reduces the complex functioning of the brain to the relationship existing between genes, chromosomes and hormones. By concentrating the focus on this single area it can be argued that there is a possibility that other variables influencing human thought and behaviour are overlooked.

## Summary of key points

In this opening chapter psychology may be likened to an 'academic ship of fools'. It is a complex discipline with competing views on how the subject ought to be studied. It is a diverse discipline with a range of identifiable 'sub-areas' of interest. There are a number of schools of psychology, each of which has adopted its own model of the person. The chapter has defined and explored five major perspectives that are of use to early years workers. Examples of specific therapies have been provided and there has been a critical appraisal of each of the therapies. It may be argued that the best way to apply psychology to early years is to combine the perspectives and their therapies in such a way that the complex needs of individuals are more likely to be met. If this is done, it produces an holistic approach to meeting individual needs. If these therapies are combined with other perspectives from health and counselling there is the further likelihood that our understanding of child development can be enhanced. It may be argued that this is the best way to apply psychology to early years. The book begins with this chapter because it can be argued that psychology is a highly useful academic subject for practitioners working with children and families. In addition to being able to be applied to individual children, there is the possibility of using psychological therapies with children and families in general. The colloquial phrase 'it's all just in your mind' is often used in order to explain why someone is unable to achieve what ought to be achieved. This implies the importance of psychology (or studying the mind) at a general level. It can be argued that academic psychology is as important an academic subject as can be if we are to meet the challenges of working effectively with children and families.

## Self-assessment questions

*Question 1*
What are the five major schools of psychology?

*Question 2*
How can early years workers apply the schools of psychology to help children and maximize their professional practice?

*Question 3*
Give an example strength and weakness of each of the psychological schools of thought?

## Moving on feature

This chapter has introduced to the schools of psychological thought. Chapter 2 introduces you to a number of key sociological perspectives. Try to think of how psychology and sociology can be applied to early years in order to meet the needs of children and families.

## Further reading

Gross, R. D. (2010), *Psychology: The Science of Mind and Behaviour*. London: Hodder Education.

An excellent textbook in terms of depth of content and analysis but the material is not always related to early years contexts.

Malim, T. and Birch, A. (1998), *Introductory Psychology*. London: Palgrave Macmillan.

An excellent textbook that is written in an accessible way and makes clear links to applying psychology to early years contexts.

Ingleby, E. and Oliver, G. (2008), *Applied Social Science for Early Years*. Exeter: Learning Matters.

A book that directly applies psychology to early years.

# 2 Sociology and Early Childhood Studies

## Chapter outline

## Learning outcomes

After reading this chapter you should be able to:

- identify what the term 'sociology' means;
- analyse some of the ways that sociology can be used by early years practitioners;
- critically appraise some of the ways that sociology can be applied to early years.

The chapter develops your knowledge and understanding of sociology and how it can be applied to the early years context. The chapter provides an introduction to sociology and explores how the discipline can be applied to early years. There are a number of sociological perspectives and each one has a particular understanding of how social factors influence individuals. This understanding is outlined, analysed and critically appraised within the chapter. The chapter adopts a similar structure to Chapter 1 as there are formative activities that reinforce learning in relation to the main sociological perspectives that are of relevance for early years practitioners.

Sociology is a discipline that attempts to explain the social world. In some respects it is similar to psychology as there have been a number of thinkers who have influenced the subject area over time. It is an important academic discipline for early years practitioners because it explains how social factors influence the development of children and families. This chapter explores some of the key perspectives within sociology. Before we look at the main sociological perspectives and discuss how early years practitioners can apply these ideas it is important to identify what the term 'sociology' means.

# Defining sociology

The word 'sociology' can evoke a number of reactions. It is a discipline that is often associated with politics, especially left-wing politics, a legacy of the influence of Karl Marx. It may also be equated with analyses of human communities and the attempts that are made to make sense of these differing social groups. A dictionary definition of sociology is that it is:

the study of companionship.

(Online Dictionary)

## Reflective Activity 2.1

What do you think this dictionary definition means? Is it similar or different to your understanding of sociology? How is it similar? How does it differ?

Feedback

This definition of sociology may explain the discipline's literal meaning. Sociologists such as Auguste Comte, Emile Durkheim, Max Weber and Karl Marx are interested in studying human communities in order to understand how they have formed, how they function and how they develop. The influential ideas of all of these sociologists rest at the centre of the main perspectives that influence the discipline. This means that we can use this dictionary definition as a starting point in attempting to understand what sociology is in order to deepen our understanding of the key perspectives that have influenced the subject.

If we develop this initial understanding of sociology we can say that sociologists are not necessarily left-wing political activists and that this is a common delusion and mis-interpretation of the discipline. The word sociology is derived from the Latin for 'associate' ('socius'). This means that the literal translation of sociology is 'the study of association or companionship'. Taylor et al. (2004, p. 1) argue that although this definition of the subject is 'limited' it still identifies the main concern of the subject. This develops the argument of the American social scientist C. Wright Mills (1959) that if we are to understand individual experiences we have to look beyond the personal circumstances in which they occur. This idea implies that personal circumstances can only be understood if they are placed within a broader context of public factors. Taylor et al. (2004, p. 2) also argue that the first wisdom of sociology is to make us realize that 'things are not what they seem'. The social world is made of a number of layers of meaning so this necessitates challenging the assumptions that may be made about the social world. It leads Berger (1966) to argue that sociology is characterized by a particular way of thinking that is reluctant to accept obvious explanations of the social world. The result is a sceptical attitude to what is viewed as being 'common-sense'. Taylor et al. (2004, p. 3) refer to Nietzsche's notion of the 'art of mistrust' to summarize this prevalent characteristic of sociology.

In addition to the stereotypical notion that sociology is 'left-wing and political' there may also be an assumption that sociologists write about the obvious in an oblique way. Durkheim's (1952) work on 'suicide' may be developed to argue that generating a sense of 'community' and 'belonging' is important in reducing suicide. Critics of this finding may argue that this is an obvious point that does not have to be presented in an academic way.

## Reflective Activity 2.2

Think about the above argument. Do you think that sociology is 'common sense written about in an oblique way'? If so why, if not why not?

Feedback

It is important to ensure that you are as open-minded as possible about any academic discipline so that you do not follow the stereotypical assumptions that can be made about certain subjects. Since sociology has become associated with challenging social assumptions it has also become equated with radical thought that is not always within the boundaries of conventional social thinking. This can mean that sociologists are regarded as being opposed to the established order. This potentially unsettling challenge can mean that sociologists are labelled in a negative way. This can be one of the reasons why the subject is criticized and derided. It is worth remembering that sociology has an enormous philosophical heritage that reformulates the ideas of Plato, Hegel, Kant and Heidegger. It may be wiser to digest the arguments of the main thinkers within sociology before assuming that the subject is characterized by 'common sense written about in an oblique way'.

We can now look at exploring some of these understandings of sociology. This adds layers of meaning to the initial explanations of how the discipline can be understood in relation to early years. Key perspectives informing the discipline will be introduced before we analyse how sociology be applied to early years.

# The sociological perspectives

Table 2.1 gives a summary of three highly influential sociological perspectives with a brief description of their key features.

These perspectives are especially important because of the influence they have had in shaping the academic concerns of sociology. Marshall (1994) argues that the ideas within the perspectives have been informed by the philosophy of Plato, Hegel, Kant and Heidegger. The Durkheimian focus upon the idea that society is greater than the individual links to the philosophy of Plato. This is because Plato has popularized the idea of the existence of an intelligence that is above and beyond the individuals within society (Audi, 1995, p. 618). The opposite idea that individuals are consciously creative so that they shape the social world links to the philosophy of Kant (Marshall, 1994,

**Table 2.1** Sociological perspectives

| School | Key features |
| --- | --- |
| Functionalism | Social behaviour is a product of 'society'. Society is regarded as being more important than individuals. This perspective has been popularized by Emile Durkheim. |
| Interactionism | Social behaviour is viewed as being generated by inventive and creative individuals. The actions of these individuals are considered to be more important than 'society'. This perspective has been popularized by Max Weber. |
| Conflict theory | This sociological perspective focuses upon economic relations within societies. These economic relations are considered to determine the nature of society. Karl Marx has made the perspective famous. |

p. 265). It is also central to Husserl's interpretative philosophy that is in turn associated with Heidegger's focus on the importance of individual experiences (Marshall, 1994, p. 213). It can also be argued that an important characteristic of conflict theory is to view social processes as being opposed to each other in a way that is similar to what has been popularized as the Hegelian notion of 'thesis, antithesis and synthesis' (Audi, 1995, p. 315). This suggests that the perspectives can be traced back to these philosophers. There follows a summary of each of the above perspectives in order to develop the definitions within the previous table. Each of the key perspectives is defined, key figures influencing the perspective are identified and central terms within each perspective are explained.

# Functionalism

Functionalists such as Emile Durkheim regard society (or societies) as being of more importance than individuals. The perspective gets its name from asking about how social institutions such as 'the family' and 'the political system' make society function. The perspective begins from the assumption that every society has a number of basic needs if it is to survive. An example of such a 'need' is the importance of social order. Functionalists consider that social order is not possible unless there are shared norms and values. These shared norms and values can only become widely accepted through socializing individuals. This means that functionalists are interested in identifying the ways that order is established within society. Durkheim is a key functionalist thinker. His work is personified in the sociology of crime and punishment in classic social science texts such as *The Division of Labour* (1984/1893), *Two Laws of Penal Evolution* (1899–1900) and *Moral Education* (2002). The primary focus for Durkheim is not so much the individual but more the whole social body in order to 'maintain inviolate the cohesion of society by sustaining the common conscience in all its rigour' (1984/1893, p. 63).

This way of visualizing society means that functionalists are interested in the social components that combine to give a society its definition. This means that social institutions such as the family, the health system, the education system and the political and religious institutions of society become critically important in establishing social order.

Functionalists are also interested in conflict and social disorder. The forces that are contrary to the established order are a part of many social systems.

Functionalists are interested in the ways in which the social system deals with negative social factors to the extent that they become a manageable part of the social world. The presence of social disorder raises a criticism of functionalism. Taylor et al. (2004, p. 15) criticize the perspective for 'presenting a deterministic picture of social behaviour'. This is because of the functionalist focus on social systems forming individuals. The reason why this functionalist approach is open to criticism rests in the social disorder that many individuals can experience. If the social system is to be omnipotent in the way that authors such as Orwell (1949) have popularized, there could never be the conscious rejection of so many social values that have been highlighted by the UK media in 2011. This suggests that if one focuses on the importance of the social system to the detriment of acknowledging the importance of creative individuals making choices, one is excluding a massively significant part of social interaction.

## Case study

The Bowman family live in an inner city council estate. Within the estate there are problems with unemployment, crime, drug and alcohol addiction. The family include Angela Bowman who is a single mother with three children (Ann (8) Michelle (7) and Dean (4)). Ann and Dean both receive support for their special educational needs. Dean has already been cautioned for aggressive behaviour at his local nursery and Ann has had a number of episodes of 'challenging behaviour' at her local school. Michelle is different to Ann and Dean. She seems to be a gentle and shy girl who is naturally good at reading, writing and numeracy. Michelle seems to be the complete opposite to Ann. Angela explains the difference between Michelle and the other children by reasoning that 'the beauty of children is that they're all different'.

### Reflective Activity 2.3

How does the case study contradict functionalism?

#### Feedback

We have said that functionalists are interested in looking at how social groups influence individuals. This means that this sociological theory emphasizes the importance of the 'big picture' as opposed to looking at how individuals create and generate social meaning. The Bowman family do appear to have been influenced by social factors. It could be argued that the challenging behaviour of Ann and Dean is a product of the negative social environment that is being experienced by the family. The difficulty of this argument is that the same social factors appear to have influenced Michelle in a very different way. Michelle is described as being 'gentle and shy'. This appears to indicate that individuals are not entirely a product of social forces. It suggests that the individual characteristics of each person may be a product of forces that are unrelated to wider social environment.

# Interactionism

Interactionists such as Max Weber focus on how individuals interact with each other. Weberian theory may be considered as being an appealing lens through which to view early years. The notion of 'verstehen' with its implication that the individual should be the primary unit of sociological analysis appears to link to much of the learner-centred pedagogy that currently is associated with early years.

Whitehead (2010, p. 6) argues that Weber's concept of verstehen can be combined with his analysis of bureaucracy to give a powerful insight into the mechanics of UK social policies. Weber (1968) explains that the word bureaucracy is of eighteenth-century origin and means 'rule by officials within organizations'. The argument is advanced that bureaucracy is the most efficient form of organization that is exemplified by precision, continuity, discipline, strictness and reliability. Weber considered bureaucracy to be an inevitable process in the eighteenth-century Enlightenment world. Allbrow (1970, p. 47) notes that one of Weber's concerns was that bureaucracy would become so large that it 'controlled the policy and action of the organisation it was supposed to serve'. Weber (1968) outlines an ideal type of bureaucracy that can be summarized as having a specialized division of labour where different individuals become responsible for specialized tasks in pursuit of organizational goals. Weber developed the view that a major feature of modern capitalist societies is the trend towards rationalization. This conveys an emphasis on what Whitehead (2010, p. 6) refers to as 'planned, technical, calculable and efficient processes' that are devoid of emotion.

In some respects this means that interactionism is opposed to functionalism. Taylor et al. (2004, p. 17) propose that within interactionism an emphasis is placed on negotiating meanings. This means that human encounters are not considered to be 'fixed'. They are visualized as being dependent on the negotiation of those individuals involved in the encounter. Whereas functionalists such as Durkheim emphasize the importance of the social system, interactionists are concerned with the negotiated meanings that develop during the process of interaction. This process is visualized as being creative as individual human actors interpret the social system in an inventive way.

Interactionism is allied to Symbolic Interactionism. This sociological perspective emphasizes the importance of how people use symbols within interaction. Speech is regarded as being a particularly important symbolic way of guiding, interpreting and making sense of interaction. Taylor et al. (2004, p. 17) are critical of this sociological perspective because of the focus on 'small-scale interaction'. This means that the implications of wider social trends are not necessarily taken into consideration. It can also mean that interactionist studies become impressionistic and localized so that they are open to the accusation that they are unable to obtain global findings.

### Reflective Activity 2.4

Think about your own personal development. To what extent do you think that your personality has been formed by the social system? To what extent do you think that your personality is a product of negotiated meanings with other social actors?

#### Feedback

A way of resolving this 'either/or' dilemma is to view your personality as having been influenced by a combination factors. In other words the person is a product of both the wider social system and negotiated meanings with other social actors. This means that neither one perspective nor the other has the complete answer to the question of how our personality is formed. Both of the perspectives are correct to draw attention to the variables influencing personal development. Their effectiveness is heightened if they are used in tandem to account for individual development.

# Conflict theory

Conflict theory has been influenced by the ideas of Karl Marx. It is a sociological perspective that is similar to functionalism because of the emphasis that is placed upon the social system. Conflict theory differs from functionalism because there is not a focus on social consensus. The perspective investigates the conflict existing within social systems as opposed to studying the factors producing social harmony. Taylor et al. (2004, p. 15) emphasize the importance of the concept 'ideology' to conflict theory. Ideology is visualized as being the beliefs and values which disguise truth and distort the reality of the social system. This ideology is considered as supporting the values of the rich and powerful. It is regarded as being opposed to the social system's poor and powerless.

Karl Marx popularized the notion of looking at the contradictory elements of social systems. Marx also popularized the terms 'infrastructure' and 'superstructure'. Whereas the infrastructure refers to all tangible aspects of the economic system, the superstructure refers to systems of belief and ideas. According to Marx, this economic infrastructure is responsible for shaping the beliefs and ideas of the superstructure. Marx also popularized the idea of social classes. The traditional Marxist emphasis is on the existence of two main social groups, a ruling class and a subject class who are considered as being in conflict with each other. Marx argues that there are fundamental contradictions within modern industrial societies such as the United Kingdom. The exemplification of such contradictory relationships can be seen in the traditional working arrangements for factories. Whereas the workers are traditionally 'on the factory floor', the factory manager is usually based in a private office. Another example of a contradictory relationship occurs with private ownership. A few powerful individuals own companies whereas the majority of the population own very little in comparison to these powerful individuals. Marx argues that the many contradictions in society produce instability and conflict. This is the rationale behind the prediction that a revolution will occur within capitalist societies so that the social order can be refined into a communist society.

Marxism is a profound and complex social theory. The emphasis on 'conflict' is testimony to the influence of Hegel's philosophical idea of the social world being characterized by 'thesis, antithesis and synthesis'. It is acknowledged that a social revolution will only occur when the working class become fully aware of the unfair contradictions that exist within the social system. The argument runs that until this realization occurs, the social system is likely to survive because of the 'false-consciousness' of the working class. It is only when the working class become fully aware of the implications of social contradictions and of the need to replace the existing social order with a communist society that a social revolution will occur.

Marxist theory explicates the view that economic change is a necessary condition of social change which, in turn, has implications for early years (McLellan, 1986). The enduring nature of Marxist analysis is summarized by Zedner's (2004, p. 80) notion of the essential components being 'power relations, economic struggle and social conflict'. If we apply the ideas of Bourdieu (who is influenced by a Marxist tradition that emphasizes the importance of the mode and conditions of economic production), it is possible to explain the presence of competing ideologies of 'best practice' in early years. Bourdieu's (1986, 1993) work can be developed to argue that early years is part of the process of 'cultural reproduction' in neo-liberal societies as the role of the education system is to replicate the values of the dominant social classes. The consequence results in conversations about early years education either perpetuating the existing educational order or conversely promoting new understandings of the purpose of early years education. The notion of the potentially volatile nature of education with its 'profits' and 'sanctions' is referred to by Bourdieu (1986, p. 62) when he says:

> Every linguistic situation functions as a market on which the speaker places his products, and the product he produces for this market depends on his anticipation of the price his products will receive. We enter the educational market with an expectation of the profits and sanctions we shall receive.

Bourdieu is arguing that although shared understandings of teaching and learning perpetuate the educational field there is also the presence of conflict in the realm of ideas about education. Bourdieu (1993) has popularized the notion of 'cultural capital' by arguing that a main purpose of the education system is to facilitate this 'cultural reproduction'. According to Bourdieu (1986, p. 34):

> In every epoch there is a constant struggle over the rate of exchange between the different kinds of capital, a struggle among the different fractions of the dominant class, whose overall capital is composed in differing proportions of the various kinds of capital.

Bourdieu regards the purpose of the education system as being to reinforce the values of the dominant classes and the 'constant struggle' that results is a consequence of the inherent contradictions that operate within unequal capitalist societies. These inherent contradictions hold the potential to produce competing ideologies that hold different understandings of the purpose of early years education.

---

### Reflective Activity 2.5

Why do you think that Marx's prediction that there will be a revolution in capitalist societies has only happened in a few capitalist social systems?

#### Feedback

It can be argued that a difficulty with the traditional Marxist focus on the economic infrastructure is that it neglects the creativity of individuals. It is too prescriptive in that the assumption is made that social contradictions will lead to a revolution and a new social order. Individuals will not necessarily react in the way that Marx predicted when there is the potential for meanings to be negotiated. The false consciousness that Marx writes about may be perpetuated when individuals are content to maintain the existing social system. Marx thought that false consciousness would lead to a revolution once the proletariat became educated and politicized. In the United Kingdom there are many people who reject politics (online at: www.guardian.co.uk). They are not prepared to be part of what is deemed to be 'spin' and 'lies'. It is not necessarily accurate to refer to this state of mind as false consciousness. It appears to be the case that individuals have a large number of choices available to them. Revolution is one possible choice that seems to be rejected because it is associated with political movements that have lost their credibility. Although there may be a significant number of people who are not as content as they could be they do not necessarily feel so discontent that a revolution is likely to result.

---

# Applying sociology to early years

The three sociological perspectives that have been introduced within this chapter can be applied to early years. They offer a number of insights into society and provide a further level of skills whereby professional practice can be informed by social theory. If this raised awareness of the importance of social factors is combined with the applied psychological theory discussed in Chapter 1, there is the possibility of an even more profound holistic therapy combining psychological and sociological ideas. This section of the chapter introduces some of the ways that you can apply sociological ideas to the early years context.

# Functionalism and early years

In the previous section of the chapter we defined functionalism as being a sociological perspective that is concerned with social systems in relation to how consensus is maintained. This macro approach focuses on the wider social picture by drawing attention to the impact of wider society on children and families. The emphasis is placed on how children and families are affected by social structures such as the education system, the health system and the political system. In the United Kingdom there was relatively little statutory support offered to children and families prior to 1946. This pivotal date is the time when the welfare state became such an important part of UK social policy. William Beveridge's notion of a welfare state looking after the needs of children and families from birth until death became a dominant idea within UK society from 1946 onwards. The welfare state led to the introduction of the NHS, social security and social services. This meant that there was a formal recognition that the wider social system has a massive impact upon the lives of children and families.

It is important for early years practitioners to acknowledge that the social system has a massive impact on the life chances of children and families. It can be argued that the relatively affluent life style enjoyed by many UK people is a product of the welfare state. This means that it is important for early years practitioners to become as fully aware as possible of the state services that are available to help children and families. As opposed to accepting that responsibility rests with individuals to be 'self-reliant' it is important to acknowledge that life chances are heavily influenced by the type of society that has been created. This argument is justified by considering the many problems that are experienced by children and families living in countries who do not have a welfare state. If the social system is underdeveloped so that individual families become accountable for their life chances there are fewer opportunities for those children and families who are unable to look after their own interests.

This means that early years practitioners need to be aware of the importance of having robust social agencies that are able to plan for and coordinate effective health care and education. This does not mean that it is necessary for early years practitioners to become political activists! It is more of a need to learn the lessons of history. The welfare state has improved the life chances of many children and families so this means that it is important to acknowledge the importance of wider social structures being able to help those who cannot help themselves.

The following case study example outlines the ways in which the functionalist awareness of the social system can be applied to early years.

## Case study

The Njemba family arrived in the United Kingdom after spending 7 years in Nairobi. Mr and Mrs Njemba have three children aged 7, 5 and 3. The family have become used to being reliant on each other because of the difficulties with the infrastructure in Nairobi. They used to live in a poor district of the city. There were no shops in this area, no running water and no school for the children until last year. A Roman Catholic missionary organization established a school for the children and the benefits of a basic education persuaded the Njembas to move to the United Kingdom. Although the family have immigrated into the country illegally they are still sure that there are many benefits to living in the United Kingdom. They are able to enjoy a much more robust infrastructure. There is running water and employment opportunities. Although the Njembas are not considered to be official UK citizens they think that they have many more social benefits living illegally in London than they ever did as legal citizens in Nairobi. The family attend mass at a local Catholic Church and their children already receive a number of social and educational benefits from being part of this religious community. Each Sunday there is a 'children's liturgy' and the children get to use pens, paper, books and musical instruments. One of the parishioners is a foreman in a local factory and he has told Mr Njemba that there is the possibility of 'casual labour'. The Njembas think that their life opportunities are dramatically different within a social system that appears to offer so many opportunities.

### Reflective Activity 2.6

How can functionalism be applied to this case study?

### Feedback

In the case study about the Bowman family we said that functionalists are not able to explain every aspect of child development because there are 'non-social' factors that also influence children. The above case study does, however, reveal the potential importance that a child's social environment can have on its development. When a social

system has a poorly developed infrastructure, this is likely to have profound consequences for the child's development. Once the Njemba family move to a society with an
improved infrastructure, there are more opportunities for the family and these opportunities (both economic and social) help the children's physical, intellectual, emotional
and social development.

## Interactionism and early years

In contrast to functionalism, the interactionist perspective emphasizes the importance of individuals. There is less focus on macrosociological structures and much more attention paid to the ways in which individuals negotiate meaning during their social encounters. This sociological perspective is important for early years because it reinforces the importance of meeting the individual needs of children. The interactionist approach to sociology would endorse any practice that aims to treat children as individuals, with the potential to grow and develop as long as this opportunity is presented to them. Even the word 'sociology' appears to emphasize the importance of studying groups of individuals as opposed to focusing on the meanings that are negotiated by social actors. To apply an analogy, it is as if the 'individual trees' are being missed because of the focus on the 'wider wood'. It can be argued that effective early years practice cannot be characterized by looking at major social structures because the individual needs of children and families are likely to be missed if this is the prevalent approach to practice. The interactionist approach to sociology begins by asking how individuals interpret the social world and in turn negotiate social meanings. If early years practitioners adopt a similar philosophy, the individual child and their rights is likely to become central to practice. This theme is emphasized in Nigel Parton's (2005) book. It is considered to be vital that children's individual needs are central to practice if quality child care provision is to be given.

If an interactionist approach to early years work is adopted it is also more likely that the creativity of children will be acknowledged and incorporated into effective practice. It can be argued that an interactionist perspective may be more prepared to value the importance of 'free-play' because of the emphasis that is put on each child nurturing their individual creativity. Play techniques that stimulate the child's imagination are also likely to be considered to be important to children's growth and development if one adopts an interactionist perspective. This is because of the emphasis that is placed on meanings being negotiated by creative individuals. Some of the benefits of an interactionist approach to early years practice are outlined in the following case study.

## Case study

Amanda has recently completed a PGCE and she is in her first teaching post in a primary school. Amanda has studied a number of educational theories and she is particularly interested in the ideas of the psychologist Howard Gardner and his concept of 'multiple intelligences'. Amanda has adapted Gardner's work to devise a questionnaire that assesses individual children's learning preferences. Amanda has used this questionnaire with children aged 6–7. She has created a learning profile for the class and this is used in order to organize teaching sessions. Amanda sets tasks for the children according to their learning preference. Amanda has found that the children have made much progress since she has been responding to their individual learning needs. As well as feeling valued, the children are able to complete tasks that appear to be appropriate to their individual needs. This positive teaching experience has made Amanda even more concerned about the National Curriculum. She considers it to be a global approach to education when it would seem to be much more important to meet individual needs.

### Reflective Activity 2.7

How can interactionism be applied to this case study?

### Feedback

We have emphasized that interactionists emphasize the importance of individuals and their ability to create and negotiate social meanings. The 'personalized learning activities' that are being applied within the case study appear to support what interactionism says. As opposed to emphasizing the importance of the social group, interactionism places an emphasis on the importance of the individual. In this case study, each learner has an individualized learning profile and this becomes the means of developing learning. It can be argued that supporters of interactionism are likely to have reservations about a 'national curriculum' that places the goals of the social group before the needs of individuals.

## Conflict theory and early years

We said in the previous section of the chapter that conflict theorists are interested in how social systems deal with social conflict. We also noted that the most famous strand of conflict theory applies the ideas of Karl Marx in explaining the social environment. This means that conflict theory has become associated with economics, in particular the ways that economic conflicts within social systems influence social interaction. This aspect of conflict theory is relevant to early years because of the relationship that exists between a child's economic circumstances and their ability to grow and develop. Although a number of factors influence child development it can be argued that economic circumstances are especially influential. We need only look at our society and the link that exists between economic wealth and children's educational achievement. Anthea Lipsett (2007) draws attention to the importance that the government have given to ensuring that the budgets that are given to schools enable them to resource 'world-class' learning and teaching. Early years practitioners need to be aware that children can only fulfil their potential if their economic circumstances support their growth and development. This means that it is important to be aware of the economic circumstances of the children we are working with. Although the United Kingdom is a relatively wealthy country there are still children who do not have a satisfactory diet. A House of Commons Work and Pensions Committee report in 2003–4 identified that 13 per cent of UK children experienced short-term poverty (1–3 years in poverty). These factors will have a massive impact upon how children grow and develop. If we adopt the philosophy of conflict theorists we can argue that if these economic circumstances are alleviated there are more opportunities for the children to reach their developmental potential.

## Case study

James is 6 and comes from an inner city housing complex. His mother is unemployed and their only form of income is 'social security'. Although James is an only child, his mother finds it very difficult to manage financially. Christmas is an especially difficult time because James is very aware of other children getting expensive presents. James is a malnourished child who often only has cereal before school. This means that he finds it difficult to concentrate in school. He does have a hot meal when he gets in from school but the quality of this food is not as good as it could be. James also feels the cold because his mother has been unable to get a warm winter coat for him. These material circumstances mean that James is unable to reach his educational potential. He likes books and reading but his access to books is limited compared to some of the other children in his class. James is also starting to show some signs of low self-esteem. He notices what the other children have and listens to them talking about what they do when they are not in school. This has made James feel that he is different. His best friend Will is going to 'Euro Disney' in the spring but James has never been on a family holiday. His mother does take him to the local park in the summer holidays but James wishes he could do something else. The world that he sees on the television appears to be very different to the reality of the life he leads with his unemployed mother.

## Reflective Activity 2.8

How can conflict theory be applied to this case study?

### Feedback

It could be argued that many of the difficulties that James is experiencing would be resolved if his material circumstances were improved. James is described as being 'malnourished' and this poor diet will influence his development. Although James may be a 'bright' child, his material circumstances may also be the main reason why he has feelings of 'low self-esteem'. Although 'materialism' may bring as many social problems as poverty, it would still appear to be the case that child development is profoundly influenced by the distribution of a country's wealth. In a situation of 'haves' and 'have nots' a redistribution of wealth can mean that child development improves and a more equalitarian society is thus produced.

## Reflective task

Think about each of the sociological perspectives outlined in Table 2.1 and suggest what would interest them about 'child poverty'.

### Feedback

Each of the sociological perspectives would explain child poverty differently. Functionalist sociologists would be interested in the threats that are posed to the social system by poverty. Threats to the social system are regarded as being 'dysfunctional'. This means that it is important for the social system to be able to activate a strategy in order to counter the negative impact of child poverty. The social system is regarded as being similar to a biological organism. It is proposed that in a way that is similar to the activation of the immune system there are ways of restoring the social equilibrium. Functionalists are interested in the ways that the social system's economy responds to child poverty. The argument would run that because child poverty produces instability, the social system will need to redirect economic resources to counter this problem. If there is no end to child poverty there is no way that the social system will be able to operate effectively. This may lead to the ultimate collapse of the social system and the establishment of a new social order.

Interactionist sociologists are interested in how social actors negotiate meanings. This understanding of sociology means that it is assumed that the consequences of child poverty will differ from one individual to the next. The perspective is interested in how individuals form creative strategies in order to negotiate social challenges. This means that interactionist sociologists would account for child poverty by saying that the problem is more or less pronounced according to the strategies that are employed by individuals. Just as there are some innovative individuals who are able to escape from the effects of child poverty, so there are also individuals who are unable to counter its effects.

Conflict theorists are interested in the social disorder that is generated by child poverty. Marxist sociologists explain child poverty as being an inevitable consequence of the capitalist economic system. This economic system places 'capital' (land, industry and money) in the hands of a few dominant individuals. This means that child poverty is experienced by the majority of the population. Conflict theorists would also argue that child poverty will be one of the reasons why the capitalist economic system will be overthrown once its extent is fully known.

## Practical task

When you are next on the internet do a word search for 'functionalism', 'interactionism' and 'conflict theory'. Try to find out more information about the main individuals who are associated with the perspectives (Emile Durkheim, Max Weber and Karl Marx). Make a note of what would interest the three sociologists about your own early years setting.

We can now complete our introductory chapter by focusing our discussion on critically appraising the sociological perspectives in terms of their value for early years.

# Critical appraisal of how sociological theory can be used by early years

As with psychology, there is no one perspective that provides all the possible answers to the questions that we may have about the social development of children. The most effective way of applying sociological perspectives to early years appears to be combining their relative merits in order to present as holistic an approach to understanding child development as possible.

## Appraising functionalism

All three perspectives highlighted in this chapter have strengths and weaknesses. The functionalist approach with its focus on 'social systems' can make the mistake of emphasizing the importance of the social system so that the actions of individuals are not fully taken into consideration. The danger of this approach can mean that the social system is depicted in such a way that it appears to be removed from the actions of individuals. This means that although it is correct to draw attention to the 'wider picture' it is also important to acknowledge how individuals manipulate the social system in a creative way in order to produce 'negotiated meanings'. Lopez and Scott (2000, p. 17) draw attention to the importance of acknowledging individual actions in 'modern societies'. This is because this social context is characterized by individuals being 'far more differentiated from one another'. Lopez and Scott (2000, p. 17) go on to say that 'social action in these circumstances is characterised by a high level of institutionalised individualism'. This means that the general functionalist focus on a macro social order is limited because it can only explain the actions of social systems as opposed to fully accounting for the actions of creative individuals.

## Appraising interactionism

It can also be argued that there are also limitations with the interactionist focus upon 'negotiated meanings'. It is important to acknowledge the impact that individuals have in generating social meaning in order to address the functionalist over-emphasis on 'social systems'. It may be suggested, however, that interactionists can be inclined to exaggerate the importance of individual interpretations of the social order. Lopez and Scott (2000, p. 29) make the important point that although 'individual minds' are important in holding 'knowledge', this knowledge is not isolated but 'shared by those who interact together'. A similar point is made by Davis (1948, p. 87):

> An individual carries his social position in his head, so to speak, and puts it into action when the appropriate occasion arises. Not only does he carry it in his head but others also carry it in theirs, because social positions are matters of reciprocal expectation and must be publicly and commonly perceived by everyone in the group.

This means that it is important to acknowledge the role that others play in generating social meaning. It can be argued that this focus is potentially lost by the interactionist concern with 'the individual' who may be seen in isolation from 'the social group'. A further criticism of interactionism concerns the implication that individuals are 'all important'. This is similar to Margaret Thatcher's phrase that 'there is no such thing as society; there are individual men, women and families'. This emphasis on the individual can come at the expense of neglecting the importance of the social system. It is an idea that goes against many aspects of good practice within early years because it is denying the important role that the social system has in helping to nurture and develop children.

## Appraising conflict theory

It is also possible to criticize conflict theory in a similar way to the other two perspectives. This is because this sociological perspective, like functionalism and interactionism can be accused as having a one-dimensional approach to explaining social systems. This is especially true with Marxist perspectives that often reduce their explanation for social phenomena to economic variables. Lopez and Scott (2000, p. 80) argue that the work of Habermas offers a potential solution to the tendency to focus on either 'the social system' or 'the actions of individuals' or 'the economy'. Habermas (1981) suggests that the social structure is influenced by both 'communicative action' and 'purposive action'. According to Habermas, communicative action corresponds to attaining mutual understanding between the participants of a social system. In contrast, purposive action is directed towards achieving goals by more independent and 'strategic and calculative ways'. This means that in addition to the shared social meanings of social systems there are also the creative interpretations of individuals who may manipulate the social system in order to realize particular goals. It can be argued that this synthesis of functionalist, interactionist and conflict theorist thought provides a potential means of resolving the 'either or' debate.

# Foucauldian shadows of power and oppression

Michel Foucault's work is often applied within social science in order to understand the nature of early years. It can be argued that Foucault places a different emphasis to studying sociology than the other three theoretical strands of sociology we have explored thus far. Foucault's work explores the nature and role of discourse and of power structures in society. Whereas Marxists like Bourdieu (1992) consider that discourse derives from and reflects the economic factors within which it is formed, Foucault (1971) regards discourse as being more formative. This means that Foucault is more concerned with what is occurring within institutions and the way that power is being exercised (Hudson, 2003, p. 134). Foucault is essentially providing a micro rather than a macro analysis by providing a dystopian account of post-Enlightenment events within which there occurs a Nietzschean will to power, oppression, disciplinary regulation and subjugation. McNay (1994, p. 5) argues that a central concern of Foucault is the way whereby the individual is formed as a by-product of discursive formations linked to the politics of power and the demand for social order.

Foucault's (1977) work develops the argument that 'discourse' or 'conversations' within society in general and within particular aspects of society such as the teaching profession are linked to changes in power regimes. This argument is made in the following (1977, p. 304) reflection:

> The judges of normality are present everywhere. We are in the society of the teacher-judge, the doctor-judge, the educator-judge, the social worker-judge; it is on them that the universal reign of the normative is based and each individual wherever he may find himself, subjects it to his body.

Foucault is arguing that power relationships depend upon current interpretations of social space. This suggests that the conversations that policy makers, teachers and learners have about early years are a reflection of changing power dynamics within social space.

We can see the usefulness of Foucault's ideas if we think about how and why early years' settings have changed over time. If we were able to get into a 'time machine' and go back to Victorian England, the classroom arrangements for children and teachers would be somewhat different to how they are today. We would probably find that the teacher's desk dominated the classroom and that the children were expected to sit at desks in rows. The walls of the classroom would possibly have paintings and images of the British Empire. Foucault would explain this arrangement of space as a reaction to the power relations of the time. Victorian society appeared to be quite formal in the sense of reinforcing the importance of the monarchy. The social institutions such as public education would reinforce this understanding of what was important for society.

If, however, we go into a classroom in a typical school in the United Kingdom today we find a different arrangement of social space. Many class-rooms have an 'open plan' arrangement with children learning in little cluster groups. The dominance of the teacher's desk is not as apparent as it would have been in Victorian times. An emphasis is often placed on cooperation and multiculturalism. This arrangement of social space again reinforces the current social order. The advantage of Foucault's work is that it helps us to see why understandings of teaching and learning change over time. The argument runs that as interpretations of power change, this in turn influences our understanding of what is acceptable and representative of 'best practice'. Today's emphasis that is placed on the importance of the learner is simply a response to changing views on what is appropriate in response to changing expressions of power. The appeal of Foucault's work rests in his combination of exploring the impact of social institutions on individuals. There is a fluidity in his thinking that appears to resolve the 'either or' focus of the functionalists and interactionists. Just as power influences individuals, so individuals can influence power. Power is never static. It changes its expression according to political and economic factors. This is why Foucault's work can be claimed to be characterized by a sense of holism and his approach to sociology is very useful for early years.

## Summary of key points

In this chapter we have seen that sociology is not 'common sense explained in an oblique way'. It is a discipline that has a rich philosophical heritage with competing interpretations of the social world. Like psychology, there are a number of sociological perspectives and each one has its own interpretation of the social world. The chapter has defined and explored three especially influential perspectives that are of use to early years practice. The particular relevance of these perspectives for the early years context has been explored and a critical appraisal of each of the perspectives has been given. As with psychology it can be argued that the best way to apply sociology to early years is to combine the perspectives so that the complex needs of individuals are more likely to be met. If this is done, it is possible to have the holistic approach to meeting individual needs that has been identified in the previous chapter. This would appear to be the best way of applying sociology to early years. The work of Michel Foucault with its emphasis on both social structures and individuals appears to be a way of applying this holistic approach to early years.

## Self-assessment questions

*Question 1*
Name three influential sociological perspectives?

*Question 2*
How can early years workers apply sociological perspectives to help children and maximize their professional practice?

*Question 3*
Give an example strength and weakness of each of the sociological perspectives that have been referred to in this chapter.

*Question 4*
How can the work of Michel Foucault be used to explain developments in early years learning and teaching?

## Moving on feature

This chapter has introduced you to the idea of 'perspectives' or 'paradigms' of sociological thought. Try to become familiar with this term. The research process chapter also deals with the idea that there are competing models of thought that shape the nature of the individual social science disciplines. This is a key term that will enrich your knowledge of social science in general.

## Further reading

Taylor, P., Richardson, J., Yeo, A., Marsh, I., Trobe, K. and Pilkington, A. (2004), *Sociology in Focus*. London: Causeway Press.
An excellent textbook in terms of clarity of content and analysis but the material is not always related to early years contexts.
Harlambos, M. and Holborn, M. (2008), *Sociology: Themes and Perspectives*. London: Collins Educational.
An excellent textbook that is written in an accessible way although the content is not directly linked to early years contexts.
Ingleby, E. and Oliver, G. (2008), *Applied Social Science for Early Years*. Exeter: Learning Matters.

A book that directly applies sociology to early years.

# Social Policy and Early Childhood Studies

**3**

## Learning objectives

After reading this chapter you should be able to:

- identify what social policy is;
- analyse how social policy impacts upon the professional practice of early years practitioners;
- critically appraise the implications of selected social policies for early years practice.

This chapter develops your knowledge and understanding of social policy and how it can be applied to the early years context. The chapter explains what social policy is and then explores how selected social policies can be applied to the early years context. There are a number of factors that have influenced the creation of social policies so these factors are considered within the chapter. The chapter follows a similar structure to the first two chapters as there are formative activities that develop your learning in relation to the main chapter themes.

Social policies are made by the state in order to regulate the social world. These policies have been influenced by politicians and other influential social thinkers over time. It can be argued that social policy is a particularly important area of interest for early years practitioners because of the extent of the influence that social policies have on the interaction that occurs between professionals, children and families. This chapter explores these themes. Before we look at the development of UK social policy and explore the impact that these social policies have had on the professional interaction of early years practitioners, it is important to consider what the term 'social policy' means.

# What is social policy?

Social policy is defined by Alcock et al. (2000, p. 1) as being *the practical application and implementation of those policies we consider to be social.* This appears to be a workable definition of social policy because social policy has direct consequences for children and families. This means that social policy is concerned with the welfare or well-being of individuals. Alcock et al. (2000, p. 2) develop this definition by arguing that UK social policy is especially concerned with five aspects of welfare. Alcock names these five areas of concern as *income maintenance and social security, health policy and services, the personal social services, education and training policy* and *employment policy and housing policy.* In terms of the academic content of social policy, Alcock et al. (2000, p. 2) argue that it is a subject that is informed by disciplines including *sociology, economics, politics, policy making* and *history.*

---

### Reflective Task 3.1

Which aspects of social policy do you consider to be especially relevant to early years?

#### Feedback

The previous explanation of the characteristics of social policy identifies five areas of particular importance. All five of these areas have implications for children and families. This means that they (income maintenance and social security, health policy and services, the personal social services, education and training policy and employment policy

---

and housing) are all particularly important for early years. One of the most important needs of any child is to develop. All five of the areas of social policy that Alcock et al. (2000, p. 2) identify are especially important for child development. It is particularly important that children live in households that have enough money to provide for their needs. It is also important to provide children with effective health, and social care, so that their educational needs are met in order to enable their future employment and social needs.

# The social policy process

If social policies are to be introduced in order to solve social problems, and if they are to be evaluated as being 'effective' one can apply a cyclical process of analysis. This is referred to by Alcock et al. (2000, p. 3) as *the policy cycle*. The process involves identifying a social need, proposing policy solutions, implementing these policy solutions and ultimately evaluating their effectiveness.

This means that social policy is not just a study of society and its problems. It is an area of study that is intimately concerned with how to act upon and improve social problems. The social institutions that are created to ensure that social problems are resolved are also of central importance to social policy. It can be argued that a central part of the social policy process is to look at the role of the state in relation to its effectiveness in providing for its citizens.

## Reflective Task 3.2

How can the 'policy cycle' of 'identifying needs, proposing solutions, implementing solutions and evaluating solutions' be put into effect within early years?

### Feedback

Chapter 6 explains the research process within social science. One of the main ways of identifying social problems is to complete research into social life in order to identify those aspects of society that are working and those areas that are responsible for generating social problems. If 'needs' are to be identified it is important to ensure that accurate research about social issues is completed. This research can be used to form the basis of the evidence that can be presented to identify the important social problems that need to be resolved. Anne Watson (2004) discusses the challenges that exist within the UK educational curriculum. It would appear that part of the

⇨

challenge of education within the United Kingdom is to produce a situation where teachers and learners have shared views on what is important and unimportant. We could propose that if a new educational curriculum was introduced into the United Kingdom that promoted social responsibility, this might help to change some of the lack of achievement that is being experienced within UK educational institutions. If this policy direction was adopted by UK educational policy makers it could be monitored and in turn evaluated in the hope of producing solutions to educational challenges.

# The concept of partnership

Anthony Giddens (2004) argues that the concept of 'partnership' characterizes Tony Blair and Gordon Brown's approach to social policy. This means that all the sectors of the 'mixed economy of care' (statutory, private, voluntary and informal) are being encouraged to work together. This interagency approach to providing what Blair referred to as *joined-up solutions to joined-up problems* has been continued in the United Kingdom by the coalition government.

## Reflective Task 3.3

Write out a definition for the statutory, private, voluntary and informal sectors of care provision.

⇨

**Table 3.1** Defining the mixed economy of care

| Sector of care | Definition | Examples |
|---|---|---|
| Statutory | The statutory sector includes all of the services that are financed and organized by the government. | Examples of statutory services include schools, the NHS and state social services. |
| Private | The private sector includes all of the services that operate to make a financial profit. | Examples of private services include private nurseries and private schools. |
| Voluntary | The voluntary sector operates according to 'good will'. | Voluntary organizations include charities such as 'Barnados' and 'Childline'. |
| Informal | The informal sector is characterized by family and friends caring for each other because of 'love' and/or 'obligation'. | Parents caring for children and friends caring for each other are examples of 'informal' care. |

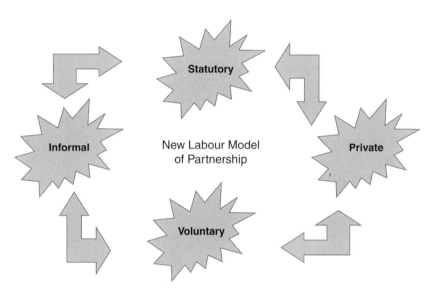

**Figure 3.1** New Labour model of partnership.

# Historical factors influencing social policy

A number of factors have influenced UK social policy from 1834 onwards. All social policies have been influenced by historical factors. In this country, ideas about society have evolved over time. This means that philosophical, economic and sociological interpretations of society have developed and informed social policy. Harris (2004, p. 1) phrases this as being the 'ideological life' that informs the social world. It can be argued that this 'ideological life' is at the centre of many of the UK's social policies.

## The 1834 Poor Law and the workhouse

Prior to 1834, the 'Speenhamland System' had been in place. The parish of Speenhamland near to Newbury in Berkshire developed the practice of giving a poor person a 'dole' or portion of bread each week and many areas of the country followed this practice. After 1834, the 'workhouse' replaced this policy. This new approach to social policy was introduced by Edwin Chadwick who criticized the Speenhamland system for being 'too generous' to the poor.

The Poor Law of 1834 represents an important development in social welfare. This policy introduced a system of 'workhouses' to address the social problem of 'poverty'. The workhouse system meant that in order to receive financial help from the state an individual had to work in an institution called a workhouse. Harris (2004, p. 52) considers the legislation to be a 'watershed in British social policy history'. This is because this social policy conflicts with previous 'laissez-faire' approaches to welfare. 'Laissez-faire' refers to the unwillingness of the state to intervene in social life. This French phrase refers to the philosophy of 'non-intervention' where individuals are 'left to do' what have they have to, in order to 'make ends meet'. This philosophy characterized the state's response to social policy within the United Kingdom prior to 1834.

Following the 1834 Poor Law, a distinction was made between the 'deserving' and the 'undeserving' poor. The legislation developed the 1601 'poor laws' that were designed to punish the 'undeserving' poor. As a result of the legislation, anyone receiving financial help from the state became a virtual social outcast. They became stigmatized, or labelled 'social lepers'. This means that the 1834 Poor Law increased the feelings of shame the individual experienced if they claimed benefits from the state. To be eligible for state help, the individual had to give up their 'personal liberty' or 'citizen's rights'.

The 1834 Poor Law is significant because it introduced an important idea in social policy, the notion of a 'means test'. The 'means test' assesses the eligibility of the claimant to receive benefits. From 1834 onwards, UK social policy makers have considered 'personal circumstances' in relation to entitlement to benefits. This notion has been encouraged by a number of influential governments. The workhouse system was based on this belief. To receive any state help a person must work in a workhouse.

**Reflective Task 3.4**

What do you think it would have been like to have been in a 'workhouse'?

**Feedback**

It is possible to imagine what it would have been like living in a workhouse if you think of the images of Victorian society that were created by Charles Dickens. The famous novel about 'Oliver Twist' portrays a world of fear, hunger, illness and poverty. The workhouse may be associated with all of these terms. As opposed to a 'caring system' that puts into effect the Rogerian principles that have been discussed in Chapter 2, the workhouse appears to be opposed to 'client-centred therapy'. The Dickensian images of society never appear to have 'disease, ignorance, idleness, squalor and want' too far removed from social life. This gives the impression that the workhouse system was wholly ineffective in meeting the needs of the poor.

# The influence of Victorian morality on social policy

Queen Victoria lived from 1819 to 1901 and was monarch at a time when Britain's foreign policy was dominated by imperialism. It can be argued that the influence of the Victorian era on social policy is important. Religion was a particularly important component of Victorian life. This led to the influence of the concept of 'Victorian morality' on social policy. It can also be argued that the popular perception was that it was important to 'work hard for a living and obey the ten commandments of the Bible'. The poor were treated with 'charity' or 'kindness'. They were given help but never too much help. This means that a 'carrot and stick' approach characterized social policy. A little was given but never too much in case the poor became dependent upon charity. This leads Harris to argue that although 'philanthropy' or charity is an important aspect of nineteenth-century social policy, *it would be wrong to ignore its limitations* (2004, p. 72).

# The importance of the institution

The Victorians designed enormous institutions to house those needing care. This meant that 'patients' became separated from the rest of society. The 'insane' were regarded as being 'morally wrong'. A family that had a child with disabilities was seen as being punished by God for some 'wrong' they had committed. It can be argued that Victorian society was a *controlling society*. Scull (1982, p. 198) reveals that the number of patients who were admitted to 'types of asylum' rose from 7,000 in 1855 to over 16,000 by 1890. This 'controlling system' is also revealed by the example of the Jeremy Bentham 'panopticon', an instrument of surveillance that was designed so that staff could see into every cell with a system of mirrors and observe every action of the person in 'care'.

As a result of this approach to social policy, many people avoided getting help from the state. A further problem was that although the Victorians built large institutions in order to 'incarcerate' those requiring care, large numbers of people still needed help from the informal sector of relatives and friends. In addition to the expense of placing patients in institutions, the 'care' that was given to these patients was based on punitive principles. Harris (2004, p. 101) argues that medical procedures were based on 'restraints and fear'. These procedures began to be applied to increasing numbers of people. By the end of the Victorian era, 8 per cent of the population aged over 65 were institutionalized in workhouses, homes for older people, or hospitals and infirmaries. This compares to fewer than 3 per cent today (Blakemore, 2003).

### Reflective Task 3.5

Why do you think the 'asylum model' has been discontinued?

### Feedback

In addition to the expense of building and maintaining large institutions, it can be argued that the 'asylum' is not the best way of caring for the mentally ill. Ken Kesey (1962) and Sylvia Plath (1963) have written about the 'harsh' regimes of 'care' that have been found in the asylums. These institutions were often located away from towns and cities as the 'mentally ill' became literally separated from society. The moral objection to this approach is that if we segregate those who have mental health needs we are 'dehumanizing' the mentally ill because we are not including them in social interaction.

## Social policy in the twentieth century: the liberal government 1906–14

The Speenhamland system and the 1834 Poor Law Act both represent important points in the development of social policy legislation. This is because many current social policies (e.g. 'Disability Living Allowance') have been influenced by this earlier legislation's theme of 'personal responsibility'.

Both examples of legislation reveal a move away from 'laissez-faire' as the state began to acquire more responsibility for the welfare of its citizens. Nevertheless, the theme of 'individual responsibility' is never replaced by a notion that the state should become responsible for its citizens.

This view began to change from the beginning of the twentieth century as the United Kingdom became involved in the 'Boer War' (1899–1902). Dutch settlers fought against the British with the escalation of military action leading to the United Kingdom implementing 'national conscription'. One third of these army recruits failed their medicals and the state of the nation's health led to increased calls for 'state intervention' in social life. The importance of 'national efficiency' became a prevalent policy theme of David Lloyd George's Liberal government. This concern with 'national efficiency' was considered alongside concern over the social unrest that was developing throughout Europe. Working-class people started to riot over the appalling living conditions in a number of European towns and cities. This led Dicey (1962, p. 53) to argue that 'nineteenth century Britain experienced a transition from Benthamite individualism to collectivism'. This signalled the beginning of the end of 'laissez-faire'.

In Germany, Bismarck attempted to prevent social disorder by introducing social policies that would help working-class people. At the beginning of the twentieth century, David Lloyd George visited Germany and took note of the German social benefits system because of the political credit that was gained by Bismarck. Lloyd George began to introduce similar reforms to Britain so that by 1911 there was the introduction of the first social insurance scheme in the form of a 'National Insurance Act'. The first part of the legislation dealt with insurance against loss of earnings through sickness and the second part dealt with unemployment insurance. These reforms may have been unpopular among employers who resented having to pay towards employees' insurance cover but they were popular among the electorate in general. Harris (2004, p. 165) comments that it was these reforms that *played a major role in laying the foundations for the development of the welfare state in the twentieth century.*

## Reflective Task 3.6

If you had lived at the time of David Lloyd George, do you think you would have been pleased that the 'Liberal Reforms' had been introduced?

⇨

> **Feedback**
>
> Your answer to the question would depend on who you are thinking of! If you were living in a poor urban district in poverty you would probably be pleased about the introduction of the Liberal reforms. Harris (2004, p. 165) lists the main reforms as being *the introduction of free school meals, the establishment of old age pensions* and *the creation of unemployment and health insurance schemes*. These reforms would have offered help and support for poor people. If you had benefited from 'laissez-faire' you might not have been so pleased about the Liberal reforms. The wealthy classes might have been threatened by the prospect of 'state welfare' because of the prospect of rising taxation. Like most social policies there are 'winners' and 'losers' according to whose view you are supporting!

## The legacy of David Lloyd George

From 1900 to 1945 British society changed in many important ways. In addition to David Lloyd George's social welfare reforms, women were allowed to vote. The country also witnessed the First World War from 1914 to 1918. This war was very different to other wars. The country's citizens suffered on a massive scale and the days of 'laissez-faire' (or lack of state intervention) could never be repeated. Previous wars had not witnessed such a huge loss of life. Winter (1986, pp. 72–3) reveals that by the end of 1918, 1.7 million British soldiers had been wounded and 723,000 had either died or been killed. This meant that the social welfare reforms of David Lloyd George gathered even more momentum. The population looked to the state to support them following a conflict that had affected most families.

## The development of left–wing socialism

From 1800 to 1900 there was a change in demography in Britain. The working classes became established in the towns and cities. Prior to this time the country was predominantly 'agrarian' as opposed to being 'industrial'. After 1800, more people moved into the major towns and cities. Law (1967) reveals that between 1801 and 1851, the number of people living in towns of more than 10,000 inhabitants increased by more than 270 per cent. These people looked for work in industry and the political movement 'socialism' developed to help support the rights of working-class people.

By 1918 we see a union between the concern for the need to have a compassionate, humane society seeking peaceful resolutions to conflict and a concern for the rights of working-class people. This led to socialism becoming increasingly important in the extent of its influence on social policy.

---

### Reflective Task 3.7

What do you think the political term 'socialism' means?

### Feedback

One way of remembering the meaning of 'socialism' is to recall the fable about 'Robin Hood' who 'took from the rich to give to the poor'! Socialism is a political idea that advocates 'taking from the rich' through taxation and 'giving to the poor' through establishing 'welfare services' such as state health, education, housing and social security. Whereas 'communism' advocates redistributing wealth from rich to poor through a social revolution, socialism supports the same idea but recommends democratic ways as opposed to revolutionary action.

---

# William Beveridge

Beveridge was a social reformer who urged Britain to create a new society in which everyone's needs would be met by the state. The tragedy of the First World War was exacerbated by the Second World War. Beveridge wanted to make Britain a 'New Jerusalem' or 'ideal state'. He aimed to do this by getting rid of what he described as key 'social evils' (disease, idleness, ignorance, squalor and want). The politicians who supported William Beveridge such as Clement Attlee believed that the way to do this was by having interventionist state policies. Harris (2004, p. 290) phrases this socialist strategy as *an essentially gradualist approach to social change.*

This meant that implementing Beveridge's social policy recommendations became the opposite of 'laissez-faire' because they required huge amounts of spending on public services. The Labour Party of the 1940s embarked upon a campaign of public spending to get rid of Beveridge's 'social evils'. This led to the introduction of the NHS and council housing. It led to the development of state education, social security and the introduction of statutory social services.

Beveridge's ideas were put into practice by a socialist Labour government in an attempt to change the nature of British society. Attlee's welfare state was based on the principle of ensuring equality of access to employment, education and social services. These interventionist policies gained momentum from

1945 to 1979. This led to the statutory sector becoming the most important provider of welfare services. This development was also influenced by John Maynard Keynes (1883–1946). From 1946 the country's politicians attempted to implement Keynesian economics. Harris (2004, p. 292) summarizes this approach to policy as *acknowledgement of the idea that it was a legitimate part of the business of government to seek to ensure a high and stable level of employment*. Keynes argued that investing in public services would lead to the creation of employment because of the need to construct staff hospitals, council houses, schools and colleges.

## The indirect problems of Beveridge's Britain

It can be argued that Beveridge's interventionist welfare policy fuelled economic inflation. As more money was borrowed by the government to finance the welfare state wages and prices rose as this additional money became utilized. The unforeseen consequences of these social policies contributed to the economic inflation experienced by the UK economy in the second half of the twentieth century. This has meant that Beveridge has been criticized for being an 'idealist' with impractical ideas of achieving 'a new Jerusalem'.

### Reflective Task 3.8

Do you agree with the idea that Beveridge was 'an impractical idealist'?

#### Feedback

You might agree with the suggestion that Beveridge was an 'idealist'. He recommended that the state should remove the 'five social evils' of disease, idleness, squalor, ignorance and want'. A society without these social evils would be 'ideal'! It can be argued that the practicalities of this approach to social welfare can be challenged. A society without disease, ignorance, squalor, idleness and want may be considered to be a 'utopia' of 'heaven on earth'. A realist might argue that this will never be possible because human societies can never be 'perfect places'.

## Social Policy, 1979–2001

Harris (2004, p. 303) argues that Mrs Thatcher's Conservatives made a number of significant changes to social policy from 1979. It could be argued that from 1979 onwards social policy moved away from state intervention and back to 'laissez-faire'. The politicians in the House of Commons gave Mrs Thatcher the 'nickname' 'Tina' (an acronym for 'There Is No Alternative'). This was because one of Mrs Thatcher's first controversial policies was to abolish 'free school milk'. Upon being criticized for this decision Mrs Thatcher allegedly retorted 'there is no alternative!' This was a signal that the days of highly interventionist government policies were coming to an end. Just as a number of complex factors led to the growth of the statutory sector, so there occurred a series of events that led to the dominance of a new philosophy of New Right Conservatism.

## The importance of Milton Friedman

Milton Friedman is the American economist associated with 'monetarism'. Friedman's economic ideas are based on the principle that it is important to regulate the money that is spent on public services in order to achieve social stability. This means that Friedman's ideas are opposed to high levels of 'state public spending'. Mrs Thatcher was influenced by this idea and her government attempted to control or regulate the amount of money spent on 'public services'. Much of Mrs Thatcher's social policy legislation was based on monetarist principles. The rationale behind this approach was that controlling public spending would reduce inflation and that this in turn would reduce unemployment.

### Reflective Task 3.9

What do you think are the strengths and weaknesses of Friedman's monetarist ideas?

### Feedback

Friedman's recommendation to control levels of public expenditure may be seen as a 'strength' if it leads to lower levels of taxation. If the population have 'more money in their pockets' they might spend this money on goods and services. This is likely to stimulate economic growth. Reducing the government's public spending can also be regarded as a potential 'strength' because it will lower the amount of money that the government has to borrow to pay for welfare services. This is also potentially beneficial for the economy. The 'weakness' of this economic strategy is that the public sector will be given fewer resources. This may mean that the standard of welfare services is reduced. This was a major criticism of Mrs Thatcher's welfare legacy.

## The NHS and Community Care Act of 1990

Mrs Thatcher's conservatives became known as 'the New Right'. They attempted to run health, education and social care services as if they were 'businesses' in order to improve efficiency and to promote independence. This legislation led to a number of important consequences for public service. The next section of the chapter outlines some of the New Right's social policy reforms.

## General Practitioner (GP) Fundholders

GP Fundholders were introduced under the New Right. This led to GPs being encouraged to apply for 'fundholding' status from the government. This meant that a GP became responsible for managing his/her own budget. The Conservatives thought that this was a good idea because it would lead to a GP having 'ownership' of the practice. This policy approach mirrored the private sector of 'managing directors' owning limited companies. The businessmen who advised Mrs Thatcher such as Lord Dearing and Lord Griffiths were influenced by the ergonomics of the American car manufacturer 'Ford'. Within 'Ford Motors' productivity was particularly high and part of the explanation that was given for this commercial success was that each worker was given much responsibility. It was argued that if GPs were given 'ownership of the process' through having financial responsibility, the quality of provision would improve. Opponents of the system argued that a two-tier system resulted, with GP Fundholders on one tier or level and everyone else on the next.

## Trust status

The 1990 legislation led to the emergence of 'NHS Trusts'. Trusts acquired financial responsibilities. They received money from the government and they then had the expectation of managing this money. As opposed to being dependent upon the health authority, 'Trusts' such as hospitals and ambulance services became responsible for their own financial performance.

## Purchasers, providers, commissioners

The emphasis placed upon financial responsibility led to a purchaser/provider model resulting. 'Purchasers' of health and care services such as GPs and social services bought care for their clients from health and social care providers such as hospitals and residential homes. The 'internal market' came into being as health, care and education became regulated by financial contracts.

## New Labour: 1997–2010

The criticisms of the purchaser/provider/commissioner model were one of the reasons why Tony Blair's 'New Labour' government swept to power in May 1997. Many UK citizens had become disillusioned with the New Right. New Labour promised that they would provide an alternative government, a 'third way' that would be a new combination of 'social compassion' and 'financial prudence'. A number of significant policy changes occurred in their first years of government.

## The end of fundholding

All fundholding ended in December 1999. The new philosophical approach of 'partnership' replaced the view that health, care and education should be run like a business enterprise. This led to a move towards 'consensus management' or management through 'cooperation'.

## The introduction of Primary Care Groups (PCGs)

This approach to health, care and education can be seen with the introduction of 'PCGs'. Shortly after New Labour's election victory, 'PCGs' became established. They comprised groups of local GPs serving a population of 100,000 patients. Their members came from GPs, representatives of social services and the voluntary sector. Their role was to meet together in order to coordinate and plan services together. Community nurses were given the role of 'commissioning' (or assessing local needs for services). This emphasis of cooperation as opposed to competition has become the dominant approach to social policy since 1997.

---

### Reflective Activity 3.10

Write an essay of between 800 and 1,000 words answering the following question:

In a summary of the government's NHS Plan the Prime Minister cited partnership as a challenge facing the NHS.

  a.  Explain the concept of Health Improvement Programmes.
  b.  Give examples of partnership in health and social care.

## Model answer

### Introduction

In this essay there are the following aims. An exposition will be given of the difficulties of having 'partnership' within the NHS. This account will be based upon the complex history of the NHS citing social, economic and political reasons as to why it is difficult to achieve partnership. After this general introduction to the issues inherent in the question there will be a description of the aims of 'Health Improvement Programmes' and a discussion of examples of partnership within health, education and social care.

The NHS was established in 1946 at an initial cost of £433 million (Moore, 2002, p. 35). It was introduced as a result of William Beveridge's attempt to turn Britain into a 'New Jerusalem', a place where social evils such as 'disease, idleness, squalor, ignorance and want' would be replaced by a kind and compassionate society. As Britain was recovering from the Second World War, Beveridge's ideals were of enormous appeal and a socialist Labour government introduced the welfare state (Harris, 2004, p. 52).

From this initial vision problems began to manifest themselves. Beveridge considered that the welfare state should look after the needs of its citizens from 'cradle to grave' but it soon became realized that such a partnership of people and state could never work. The Health Minister Aneurin Bevan resigned from his post as prescription charges were introduced. As each year passed, the NHS became more expensive and by the 1950s Britain was financially bankrupt, a fact acknowledged by Harris (2004, p. 300). It may be argued that the NHS has become a complication to British society in that although it is considered as being important for society it is difficult to put into action.

This has led to the New Labour government of Tony Blair and Gordon Brown attempting to introduce what Giddens (2004) refers to as a 'third way' of policies that encourage cooperation. As health and social care costs have continued to grow, an emphasis is placed upon health and social care services working together. This point is illustrated through the establishment of Health Improvement Programmes, PCGs and the cooperation between private and statutory sectors.

### a. Explain the concept of Health Improvement Programmes

Health Improvement Programmes resulted following the 1997 White Paper 'The New NHS: Modern and Dependable'. Their main aim is to reduce inequalities in health. Large-scale health inequalities have resulted in health authorities being required to publicize what they are doing to improve health. The aims of Health Improvement Programmes include overcoming inequalities, modernizing services, planning effectively and working with the voluntary sector and other organizations. It can be argued that local Health Improvement Programmes have benefits. These include greater sharing of resources among GPs, social workers, hospital consultants, pharmacists and health visitors. This point is supported by Giddens (2004, p. 82).

The advantage of this approach is that the partnership being advocated will be a way of overcoming some of the practical difficulties experienced by the NHS. In a time of financial difficulty there is professional sharing and cooperation as well as an awareness of the need to supply detailed information about improving targets.

### b. Examples of partnership in health and social care

One of the most important examples of partnership in health and social care are PCGs. PCGs were introduced in 1999. They replaced the 'GP Fundholding' model. They differ from this approach to health care in that an emphasis is placed upon cooperation and consensus as opposed to competition. Whereas GP Fundholders acted more independently, PCGs comprise all local doctors serving a local population of 100,000 people. They meet together and plan the primary health requirements of the local population. An especially important way in which partnership results is that nurses are crucially involved in 'commissioning' or 'assessing' local needs.

A further example of partnership is the 'mixed economy of care'. As opposed to one sector of provision, the private, statutory, voluntary and informal sectors now work in partnership. This theme was recently emphasized by Tony Blair in his vision of an NHS that works alongside the private sector. It is also a theme that is realized with the emphasis placed on finding 'joined-up solutions to joined-up problems'.

### Conclusion

In answering this question there has been reference made to the complex social, economic and political factors that meant a 'free' welfare state became an impossible dream. Spiralling costs have meant that today's politicians have had to reconsider their approach to social policy. There is now a focus upon partnership and consensus management. This point is illustrated through the development of Health Improvement Programmes, PCGs and the mixed economy of care.

# The 'partnership approach' to social policy and early years

The previous section of the chapter has outlined the origins of the idea of 'partnership'. In the United Kingdom, New Labour and the coalition government are unable to return to the days of 'tax and spend'. To do so would risk a return to the economic problems that the United Kingdom experienced between 1945 and 1979. It is also not likely that UK governments will mirror Mrs Thatcher's social policies. Tony Blair, Gordon Brown and the coalition government were voted into power because they presented an alternative vision of social policy to the New Right. This means that the concept of 'partnership' is likely to continue to be an important component of social policy. A number of consequences impact upon early years. This section of the chapter considers four examples of how 'partnership' is put into practice within early years by looking at some interesting areas of social policy and early years that have been discussed in the United Kingdom in recent years. Four themes are amplified through consideration of some of the policy implications of Every Child Matters, mentoring, multiple intelligences and ICTs (Information Communication Technologies) and early years.

## Every Child Matters

It can be argued that 'Every Child Matters' is one of the most influential aspects of social policy for early years. It attempts to address what Michelle Binfield (2006) refers to as 'an unwillingness to address a multiplicity of needs' (online at: www.communitycare.co.uk). 'Every Child Matters' was published in 2004. The legislation resulted from the inquiry into the death of Victoria Climbié. 'Every Child Matters: Change for Children' represents the government's formal attempt to ensure that 'children aged 0–19' are 'protected'.

## Key legislative features

Every Child Matters has five main aims. The legislation reveals the government's commitment to ensuring that every child in the United Kingdom is 'healthy, safe, enjoys life and achieves/makes a positive social contribution, and achieves economic well-being'. The key theme of the legislation is that the five main legislative aims can be achieved if 'integrated services for children' are ensured. This key point emphasizes the importance of statutory, private, voluntary and informal children's services working together through partnership. The cooperation between 'local and central children's services' is also seen as being an integral component of 'effective children's services'. This process involves 'planning, implementing and assessing the effectiveness of children's services'.

## Strengths and weaknesses of Every Child Matters

Every Child Matters is an example of a New Labour policy that attempts to improve the quality of life of children and families. It can be argued that this is in itself a worthwhile aim. Lumsden (2005) implies that the partnership approach with its emphasis on 'collaboration' does facilitate a model of 'coming together to solve problems' by providing integrated services. It can be argued that a weakness of Every Child Matters rests within its over ambitious aims. The BBC documentary 'When Satan Came to Town' (2006) reveals the difficulty of child protection because of the complex nature of child abuse cases. This may mean that it is impossible to ensure that every child in the United Kingdom is 'healthy, safe, enjoys life and achieves, makes a positive social contribution, and achieves economic well-being'.

---

### Reflective Task 3.11

Give a critical appraisal of 'Every Child Matters'.

#### Feedback

It is difficult to be critical of any policy that represents an official commitment to child protection. Every Child Matters reveals that New Labour are officially acknowledging the importance of protecting children. This in itself is a laudable aim. It is also interesting to note that the five aims of Every Child Matters are similar to Beveridge's attempt to remove the five social evils ('disease, idleness, squalor, ignorance and want') from UK society. It can be argued that this philosophy of society is good in principle. The extent to which the approach will work in practice is, however, debatable. Alcock et al. (2000, p. 323) argue that New Labour's *creation of a new welfare consensus is, at this stage, only a partial one*. This is because legislation alone does not bring an end to social problems such as 'child abuse'. It is challenging enough to ensure that all early years professionals know what 'Every Child Matters' represents, but it is even more challenging to put the legislation into effect within every early years context.

## Mentoring

Alcock et al. (2000, p. 321) argue that a main feature of New Labour's approach to educational policy is to *reinforce a greater role for parents*. This indicates that the traditional model of educational power has changed. As opposed to emphasizing the autonomy of educational professionals, the focus is placed on a more equalitarian approach to education in which educators work alongside other professionals, children and families to enable what Alcock et al. (2000, p. 321) refer to as *joined up solutions to joined up problems*. This has meant that 'mentoring' has become an important component of professional work.

In this context, mentoring can be understood as meaning 'the support given by one (usually more experienced) person for the growth and learning of another' (Malderez, 2001, p. 57). From 2005 onwards, an emphasis has been placed on the importance of mentoring so that novices are 'nurtured' by more experienced 'experts'. This point is supported by the Department for Education and Skills (DFES) research of 2006 that has investigated how the mentoring role within early years can be clarified so that early years mentoring can become more effective.

## Strengths and weaknesses of mentoring

It can be argued that the 'joined up solutions' approach to 'joined up problems' within education is worthwhile. This point is supported by Brookes (2005, p. 43) who argues that the importance of mentoring was identified by Bell and Lancaster in 1805. In other words, an effective mentoring system has been identified as being an important component of education for many years. It can be argued that effective early years education is likely to benefit from applying 'the lessons of experience'. This means that there is nothing wrong with the principle of emphasizing the importance of mentoring. What becomes more questionable is if mentoring is being recommended as an integral part of education yet there is no clear understanding of the model of mentoring that needs to be introduced. This is reported in the research of Ingleby and Hunt (2008), Ingleby (2010, 2011) and Tedder and Lawy (2009). It appears to suggest that although mentoring is emphasized as being an important component of collaboration and partnership, the mechanisms for introducing and applying mentoring into education are unclear and ambiguous.

## Reflective Task 3.12

Give a critical appraisal of New Labour's 'mentoring' policy.

### Feedback

It can be argued that 'social policy' becomes 'ineffective' if it is nothing more than 'window-dressing'. In other words, if all the policy does is to 'look good on the outside' it will never meet complex needs. This may appear to be the case with 'mentoring'. It is a policy approach that 'makes sense on the outside'. It appears to be a 'good idea' until one asks questions about how mentoring is to be effectively implemented. The Ingleby and Hunt (2008) research raises five issues about the effectiveness of mentoring. These points are: the role of the mentor needs clarification; mentors need to be more aware of the educational aims of academic programmes; uncertainty is present over mentor training needs; mentor training is inconsistent; and professional boundaries between mentors and mentees are underdeveloped. This appears to suggest that the policy of mentoring can only become a part of 'collaboration' and 'partnership' if these questions are answered.

## Multiple intelligences

Alcock et al. (2000, p. 321) argue that New Labour's partnership approach to society emphasizes the importance of 'values of community, responsibility and social solidarity'. A consequence of this approach within education is to view educators and those being educated as 'working together'. This has had consequences for those who would have previously been unable to adjust to the demands of the educational system, for example children with 'challenging behaviour' and 'special educational needs'. The consequence of the partnership model is that as opposed to excluding children who cannot meet the demands of the education system, another approach is needed. This requires the education system to adapt to the needs of children who have previously been excluded.

A consequence of this approach is the implementation of learning strategies that are based on the ideas of Howard Gardner (1984, 1993, 2000). Gardner proposes that there are eight forms of intelligence. These are 'visual spatial', 'linguistic', 'logical mathematical', 'musical', 'bodily kinaesthetic', 'interpersonal', 'intrapersonal' and 'naturalistic' intelligence. Supporters of Gardner's ideas argue that the traditional educational system is based on 'linguistic' and 'logical mathematical' intelligence. The argument runs that the educational system can be more inclusive if it acknowledges other categories of intelligence and in turn incorporates activities to develop these 'other' skills and abilities. This has led to the introduction of 'learning inventories' that attempt to identify the preferred learning style of groups of learners.

## Strengths and weaknesses of 'multiple intelligences'

The attention that has been given to multiple intelligences can be seen as being positive if it leads to a more innovative curriculum for early years. Frank Coffield's (2004) research into learning styles does acknowledge that there are potential benefits in establishing learning inventories. This allows the possibility of tailoring teaching and learning in order to meet the needs of the learners. As opposed to making the curriculum an aspect of education that is 'followed by the learners', increased awareness of learning styles can allow for more innovative teaching and learning activities. If the group's learning preference is predominantly 'visual spatial' this can be used to justify 'visual spatial' learning activities. Coffield's (2004) research also gives a critique of learning styles. It is possible to ask 'why are there eight types of intelligence?' Why not nine or ten or more? Another critique of the implementation of learning inventories is that it adds on another layer of bureaucracy to the heavily bureaucratic teaching profession. This may mean that being aware of learning styles becomes more of an aspect of 'audit' to impress education inspectors than an innovative part of the educational curriculum.

### Reflective Task 3.13

Give a critical appraisal of recent governments' acceptance of 'multiple intelligences'.

### Feedback

Coffield's (2004) research appears to question the validity of the concept of 'multiple intelligences'. This argument can be developed to question the nature of the educational policy-making process. Critics of educational policy making such as Lucas (2007) argue that too much education is 'standards driven'. This means that the educational process is not being fully acknowledged. The literal meaning of the word 'education' implies that the individual is enabled to see the world differently. This is less likely to happen if education is being 'standards driven'. If multiple intelligences are applied to education to impress inspectors, this will not mean that they become an integral part of learning. They are instead akin to bureaucratic tasks that are standards-driven as opposed to being designed to educate individuals in the truest sense of the term. Coffield (2004) argues for a return to the notion of 'Platonic kings', in other words, for educationalists who are experts in practice and in turn able to shape educational policies. Perhaps this idea should be at the centre of future early years educational policies?

## ICT and early years

There has been interest in how ICTs are used within pedagogy in early years and how policies can be developed to enhance this aspect of professional practice. Interest has been expressed in the understanding of ICTs that is applied by practitioners. A limited definition of ICTs focuses on learning with computers as opposed to a broader understanding that applies cameras, video, virtual worlds and mobile devices to learning and teaching with children aged up to 8 years. This links the policy discussion to some of the debates over the extent to which children aged up to 8 years should experience their world through the mediation of electronic media. Whereas Bers (2008, 2010) recommends the use of innovative virtual worlds in order to promote children's cognitive development in early years, Cook (2004) draws attention to some of the reservations that are expressed about using ICTs with young children. Cook (2004, p. 161) makes reference to the 'inappropriate use of ICTs' that can occur if 'computers are used to keep children busy, as a reward or motivating tool or simply to practise skills'.

## Strengths and weaknesses of ICTs

Drotner et al. (2008), Marsh et al. (2005), Plowman and Stephen (2005) and Yelland and Kilderry (2010) draw attention to the difficulty of adopting the view that ICTs are either 'good' or 'not good' for pedagogy with children aged up to 8 years. As Plowman and Stephen (2005, p. 147) argue, the evidence base for making a judgement on the benefits of pedagogy that applies ICTs to early years needs to be based on empirical study as opposed to being based on assertion. The irony appears to be that although there are practitioners who appear to value the importance of ICTs as a vital aspect of their professional development, they may equate ICTs with 'computers'. Moreover the practitioners' sense of the pedagogical importance of computers appears to reinforce Clegg et al.'s (2010) argument that ICTs have come to be regarded as an educational priority by neo-liberal countries such as the United Kingdom.

A number of recent studies (Drotner et al., 2008; Marsh et al., 2005; Plowman and Stephen, 2005; Yelland and Kilderry, 2010) have discussed the application of ICTs to learning and teaching within early years. These studies appear to suggest that there are both benefits and disadvantages to applying ICTs to pedagogy in early years. Plowman and Stephen's (2005, p. 147) definition summarizes the range of audio-visual devices, 'smart' toys, remote control devices, televisions, photocopiers, fax machines, televisions and computers that are encompassed in the abbreviation ICTs. This broad definition of ICTs includes mobile phones, laptops, cash registers, microwave ovens and barcodes. The above authors all explore how ICTs can enhance learning within early years as well as considering the understanding and application of ICTs by practitioners.

Plowman and Stephen (2005, p. 147) discovered that the 14 practitioners in their study tended to lack confidence with ICTs. This need to promote the pedagogical application of ICTs by early years' practitioners is also reinforced by Yelland and Kilderry (2010) in their longitudinal research study over 3 years with two Australian schools, 22 teachers and the children in their classes. Yelland and Kilderry (2010, p. 104) argue that many of the mathematics activities that are facilitated in the traditional curriculum focus on acquiring knowledge and building up a skills base. This empirical research identifies that the traditional curriculum in mathematics requires much teacher-led activity that gets the children to practice activities. Yelland and Kilderry (2010, p. 102) refer to this style of pedagogy as being characterized by 'unidimensional' thinking. The authors recommend transforming this unidimensional thinking into multidimensional learning through enabling the children to apply ICTs in order to explore mathematical concepts in a more creative way. This recommendation is exemplified with a learning activity about 'biodiversity' in which children are asked to 'design a garden' involving mathematical tasks using ICTs as opposed to completing unidimensional activities that are teacher led. The study suggests that ICTs do have potential benefits for learning and teaching in early years but that applying ICTs to pedagogy in early years does not just mean allowing the children to do what Plowman and Stephen (2005, p. 149) refer to as 'playing with the computer'. Plowman and Stephen's (2005, p. 153) study of seven early years settings in Scotland identifies that although ICTs have the potential to enhance children's learning, the low level of practitioner confidence with ICTs restricted the application of this form of learning. Moreover, the practitioners in Plowman and Stephen's (2005) study appear to associate computer skills with their perceived value for future schooling and employment.

This view appears to reinforce Clegg et al.'s (2010) argument that ICTs are portrayed by governments as a vital component of neo-liberal British education. It is argued that ICTs are associated with what Clegg et al. (2010, p. 41) refer to as a 'high skills strategy' that is regarded as giving the national economy a competitive edge in the global market (Coffield, 1999; Schuller and Burns, 1999).

## Reflective Task 3.14

Do you think that pedagogical social policies should encourage children to learn using ICTs?

### Feedback

It could be argued that ICTs are a means of stimulating the child's imagination and a vital part of learning. This suggests that ICTs are potentially good for pedagogy and an important aspect of social policy if teaching and learning in early years is to develop. It is also of interest that Plowman and Stephen (2005) identify that practitioners may lack confidence when they are using ICTs with children. This 'lack of confidence' may result in the practitioners using ICTs in a limited way. In other words, social policies depend upon those who are applying the policies. Governments may advocate using pedagogy that has an ICT base but if the practitioners are lacking confidence in applying technology this can also influence the effectiveness of the policy.

## Practical task

When you are next on the internet do a word search for 'Every Child Matters', 'mentoring', 'multiple intelligences' and 'early years and ICT'. Try to find out more information about these three aspects of social policy. Make a note of how the three areas of policy affect your own early years setting.

## Summary of key points

In this chapter we have seen that social policy is an important component of early years. Like psychology and sociology it is a discipline that has a rich heritage with complex socio-political and economic factors influencing the formation of differing social policies. The many complex aspects of UK society have influenced the social policies that are designed to regulate the social world. The chapter has explored four themes within social policy that are influencing early years practice. The particular relevance of these policies for the early years context has been examined and a critical appraisal of each of the policies has been given. The concept of partnership and collaboration has been explored. These concepts can be understood if one looks at the wider context of social policy. It can be argued that the complex heritage of New

Labour and the coalition government accounts for the focus on collaboration and partnership. It can also be claimed that all of these policy directions have fascinating implications for the early years context.

## Self-assessment questions

### Question 1
What is the key policy theme of New Labour and the coalition government?

### Question 2
Name four recent areas of policy interest that are affecting the early years context.

### Question 3
Give an example strength and weakness of New Labour's approach to social policy.

## Moving on feature

This chapter has introduced you to the idea of 'partnership' or 'collaboration' within social policy. Try to become familiar with this term. When you are thinking of doing research you might want to select an aspect of 'partnership' within early years as your research question. This will make your academic work directly relevant to the policies of recent and current governments.

## Further reading

Alcock, C., Payne, S. and Sullivan, M. (2000), *Introducing Social Policy*. Harlow: Prentice Hall.
An excellent textbook in terms of detail and critical appraisal but the material is not always related to early years contexts.
Waller, T. (2005), *An Introduction to Early Childhood: A Multidisciplinary Approach*. London: Paul Chapman.
An excellent textbook that is effectively organized and makes clear links to early years contexts.

# Pedagogy and Early Childhood Studies

**4**

## Learning objectives

After reading this chapter you should be able to:

- identify key theories of learning (behaviourism, cognitive theory and humanism) in order to help you to plan learning activities in early years;
- apply Bloom's taxonomies of learning to create effective, differentiated learning outcomes;
- explore key strategies for effective communication in the classroom.

# Introduction

This chapter links with Chapter 1 as there is the practical application of psychology to learning and teaching in early years. The chapter explores example learning theories and considers how the theories can be applied to education in the classroom. A main theme of the chapter is to consider how pedagogy is informed by key learning theories. The consideration of theory and how it can be applied to practice will in turn help you with your curriculum planning and wider learning experiences. The application of Bloom's 'taxonomies of learning' model will help you to identify the importance of having clear, differentiated learning outcomes set at different levels in order to enable the facilitation of learning. The final section in this chapter explores key strategies for effective communication in the classroom. Effective communication skills are important if we are to facilitate learning in early years. This aspect of pedagogy is important for education in general and requires us to reflect on the development of the children's general communication skills.

# Educational psychology

Educational psychology is the study of how humans learn in educational settings. The discipline explores the effectiveness of educational interventions, the psychology of teaching and the social psychology of schools as organizations. Educational psychology is concerned with how students learn and develop. Educational psychology can be understood through its relationship with other disciplines. The discipline in turn informs a wide range of specialities within education studies, including planning learning, educational technology, curriculum development, education for students with learning difficulties and disabilities and classroom management.

We can explore educational psychology in this chapter by defining, comparing and contrasting different types of behavioural learning theories. These theories include learning by association (classical and operant conditioning), cognitive theory and humanist theory. The learning theories can be explored through considering how each theory can be applied to pedagogy in early years.

# Theories of learning: behaviourism

According to behaviourists such as Skinner, learning is regarded as being a relatively permanent change in behaviour brought about as a result of experience or practice. Behaviourists recognize that learning is an internal event. Learning, however, depends upon the display of overt behaviour.

## Learning by association

The term 'learning theory' is often associated with behaviourism. The focus of the behavioural approach is on how the environment impacts on overt behaviour. This makes behaviourism different to other explanations for learning such as 'biological maturation' or 'genetics' due to the emphasis that is placed on the importance of the environment.

If we are asked to think of a marketing logo we can probably think of a brand name and see the image 'in our head'. We are so used to seeing these images in the media and around our daily environment that we do not need the company name to recognize what is being advertised. This is because we have learnt the company name through association. We now associate the logo/picture with the organization. How many more pictures do you see on a daily basis that you do not need an explanation or title to recognize?

Advertising can play a significant role in conditioning us. The media and marketing groups pair a stimulus (the product) with a conditioned response. This means that a new car (a neutral stimulus) is associated with a positive conditioned stimulus (models, fun and holidays for example). Summer holidays are advertised with good weather, lovely beaches, nice hotels and the image of having a good time. The reverse can also happen, in other words creating negative associations such as in political advertising (pairing something unpleasant with a particular party).

## Examples of learning by association and education

An example of learning by association and education can occur if children learn a particular subject because they unconsciously associate it with a teacher they like. Another example of learning by association is when teachers follow particular routines in order to show the children what they are expected to do. A teacher may stand in a particular area of the classroom in order to get the children's attention. A particular form of music may be played in order to get the children to go quiet. Learning through use of mnemonics is a further example of learning through association. This may take the form of associating a 'difficult' spelling with a phrase or sentence, so for example the word *science* could be broken down into:

*Science Can Interest Every Nosy Child Everywhere.*

## Classical conditioning

Classical conditioning is a type of learning that is associated with the behaviourist school of thought. As behaviourism is one of the earliest pedagogical learning theories it is referred to as a classical theory. One of the main theorists who is associated with the development of classical conditioning is Ivan Pavlov, a Russian scientist trained in biology and medicine. Pavlov studied the digestive system of dogs and he became intrigued with the observation that dogs deprived of food began to salivate when one of his assistants walked into the room. Pavlov began to investigate this phenomenon and established the laws of classical conditioning.

During Pavlov's investigations he discovered that an 'unconditioned stimulus' (e.g. food) will naturally (without learning) elicit or bring about an 'unconditioned response' (e.g. salivation). Pavlov's studies with dogs revealed that a natural response occurs to an unconditioned stimulus. However over time this unconditioned stimulus can combine with other factors in order to elicit what is referred to as a 'conditioned response'. If, for example a dog is given food every time a bell is rung, the dog will eventually salivate when the bell is rung. The food is the unconditioned stimulus and the salivation is the reflexive response. When the dog salivates upon hearing a bell this represents an example of a 'conditioned response' to a 'conditioned stimulus'. The bell is the conditioned stimulus and the salivation is the conditioned response.

If we apply this theory to the early years classroom, classical conditioning is seen primarily in the conditioning of emotional behaviour. Factors influencing our emotions become associated with neutral stimuli that gain our attention. For example, the school, classroom, teacher or subject matter are initially neutral stimuli that gain attention. Activities at school or in the classroom automatically elicit emotional responses and these activities are associated with the neutral or orienting stimulus. After repeated exposure to the stimuli, the previously neutral response will elicit the emotional response.

*Example:*

- A child is bullied at school.
- The child feels bad when bullied.
- The child associates being bullied with school.
- The child begins to feel bad when they think of school.

In order to extinguish the association of 'feeling bad' and 'thinking of school', the connection between school and being bullied must be broken.

# Operant conditioning

Operant conditioning can be defined as a type of learning in which behaviour is strengthened if it is followed by a 'reinforcer' (reward) or diminished if followed by a 'punishment'. Operant conditioning tends to be associated with situations in which a choice of behaviour is possible. Operant conditioning techniques attempt to regulate the choices being made by the individual. A central aspect of operant conditioning is consideration of the ways in which the environment produces consequences. It is important to distinguish between the 'who' and the 'what' that is being 'reinforced', 'punished' or 'extinguished'. Additionally, reinforcement, punishment and extinction are not terms restricted to experiments. Naturally occurring consequences can also be said to 'reinforce', 'punish' or 'extinguish' behaviour and these consequences are not always delivered by people. 'Reinforcement' causes behaviour to occur with greater frequency whereas 'punishment' results in behaviour occurring with less frequency. 'Extinction' refers to the lack of any consequence following a type of behaviour. When behaviour is inconsequential, producing neither favourable nor unfavourable consequences, it will occur with less frequency. When a previously reinforced behaviour is no longer reinforced with either positive or negative reinforcement, it leads to a decline in the response. One of the psychologists associated with operant conditioning is Burrhus Skinner. Skinner believed that internal thoughts and motivations could not be used to explain behaviour. Instead, he suggested, we should look at the external, observable causes of human behaviour.

## Skinner's box

In operant conditioning, the subject's behaviours are reinforced by desirable results, punished by undesirable results or extinguished by having no result. Reinforced behaviours will occur more frequently, while punished and extinguished behaviours will be performed less often. An example of operant conditioning is a rat learning to navigate a maze more quickly and efficiently after a number of attempts. A 'Skinner box', used to study these concepts, is a box that houses an animal such as a rat and offers both unconditioned and conditioned stimuli – such as coloured lights and food, respectively – and response levers or keys that serve to monitor the animal's behaviour. A Skinner box may be used to test classical conditioning in a bird by associating a red light with each 'feed', eventually causing the bird to peck not only at food, but upon seeing the red light. A Skinner box may be fairly simple, with only one lever or key, or it may be quite complex, with a variety of stimuli and ways of monitoring responses. The Skinner box has received criticism because it does not capture every aspect of the animal's behaviour. Pushing the lever with a nose or a paw registers as the same response, for example, and light touches of the lever may not be recorded.

### Applications of operant conditioning

**Superstitious behaviour**

Superstitions that are reinforced can have a similar effect, in other words some people believe it is dangerous to walk under a ladder. If they attempt to walk under a ladder and a negative response occurs (e.g. they trip and fall) their superstition will become stronger, however if they walk under a ladder and then win the lottery the superstition will obviously no longer have the same negative response.

**Behaviour management**

We can use a 'punishment' to manage classroom behaviour for example if a child is constantly late for class, you may want to use a negative reinforcement such as 'no break' or 'missing ten minutes of their lunch time break'. If this strategy is adhered to for all the children who are late, the inappropriate behaviour is likely to decrease.

## Pedagogy based on behaviourism

- Teaching by shaping desired behaviour – rewards and punishments.
- Being a role model by personifying appropriate behaviour.
- Tests – often involving memory (remember the mnemonics).
- Step-by-step approaches to learning.
- Breaking big tasks into bite size tasks, in order to allow for frequent experiences of success.

- Quick feedback in order to motivate the children.
- Demonstrating how to complete tasks.
- Allowing learners to practice.

# Operant conditioning pedagogical overview

If behaviour is reinforced it is more likely to be repeated. If you are applying operant conditioning to teaching in early years, it is important for reinforcement to follow the desired behaviour as soon as possible. It is also important to ensure that consistency characterizes the behaviour programme if it is to be a success.

## *Positive reinforcement*

We can provide positive reinforcement when we are teaching in early years in a variety of ways. These ways can include verbal praise, giving good grades for good work and using non-verbal cues (head nodding, smiling, raising eyebrows).

## *Negative reinforcement*

We can also reinforce behaviour in 'negative' ways by offering a 'threat' or 'punishment'.

## *Punishment*

Punishing children is not associated with 'best practice'. This is because the general pedagogical ideal is that children should be learning 'what to do' as opposed to 'what not to do'.

## *Teaching activities applying operant conditioning*

There are a number of example teaching activities that apply operant conditioning. Some of these activities include the following:

- 'Skills and drills' (repetitive exercises) using worksheets.
- 'Programmed instruction' through memorizing information.
- 'Role play' (realistic practice) through modelling.
- Multiple choice questions that practice key skills.
- Step-by-step approaches exemplified by teacher talk.
- 'Token economies' where positive behaviour is rewarded by receiving a desirable token such as a desirable 'badge' and punished through denying the child the token.

## *Applying operant conditioning in the classroom*

Children can be influenced by their classroom experiences in a profound way. The following recommendations are based on the application of principles of operant conditioning.

- It is important to stress key points by summarizing at the beginning and end of classes.
- It is also important to praise and encourage (past success provides motivation for present learning!).
- Make sure that you set clear objectives and use these to measure students' achievement.
- Allow time for practice, not just theory.

## *Criticisms of behaviourist approaches to teaching*

There are a number of criticisms of behaviourist educational approaches. These include:

- Behaviourist education tends to be teacher-led and centred on the teacher.
- This may generate a passive view of the children as learners because they are regarded as being 'shaped by the learning environment'.
- The application of operant conditioning techniques such as token economy can be regarded as being authoritarian because the teacher is essentially manipulating the learning process. This can represent a disempowerment of the learner.
- External reinforcement is used to motivate learners as opposed to encouraging internal motivation. This approach to learning can in turn remove freedom from the learning process.

# Cognitive learning theory

> ## Reflective Task 4.1
>
> - Think of a number between 1 and 10.
> - Double the number.
> - Add 8.
> - Half the number.
> - Subtract the original number from the new number.
> - Give the number a letter: 'A' for 1, 'B' for 2, 'C' for 3, 'D' for 4, 'E' for 5, etc.
> - Think of a European country that begins with the letter.
> - Think of an animal you might see in a circus that begins with the second letter of the European country!
>
> (answer follows)

Cognitive theory is based on the premise that there are thought processes behind human behaviour. An important component of cognitive theory is the Gestalt theories of perception that explore how the brain imposes patterns on the perceived world. The Gestalt theories of perception are often associated with problem-solving learning. Cognitive theory is also influenced by the developmental psychology of Piaget through focusing on the maturational factors that influence human understanding. Broadly speaking, cognitive theory is interested in how people understand the world around them and in their aptitude and capacity to learn. Cognitive theory is also interested in learning styles and it is the fundamental basis of the educational approach known as constructivism. This aspect of education emphasizes the role of the learner in constructing his or her own ideas and the factors influencing this process.

### *Answer to fun activity!*

Were your answers Denmark and Elephant? This is because you have already learnt that Denmark is a European country beginning with D and an Elephant is perhaps one of the few zoo animals beginning with E! You have used your cognitive memory skills to identify the answers.

## Memory

The 'memory' is a very complex human function that is much researched and of tremendous interest to cognitive theorists. Memory is also of central importance to learning. Indeed, learning depends upon the memory with the process of 'memorizing' being part of one of the lowest levels of rote learning. Memorizing begins with a sensory buffer. Part of the information being memorized stays in the brain for about 1/15th of a second, while the brain assembles it to 'make sense'. Most of us will have experienced the illusion by which a succession of still pictures presented rapidly enough appears to be moving as it is the basis of all cinematography. Once the frame rate drops below about 16 frames per second, however, we may well become conscious of the flicker or jumps from one still image to another. Similarly, we do not hear a succession of speech sounds, but complete words or phrases. It is as if the brain waits to assemble a meaningful sound before passing it on to the next stage which is short-term memory (STM). The human STM appears to deal best with sounds rather than visual stimuli, but this may be due to the fact that visual stimuli are taken in all at once, whereas sounds are processed in a linear fashion – over time. In actual fact the STM is able to hold material for about 15–30 seconds, although this can be expanded by practice. This is much shorter than we may initially realize. In general, the human memory has a capacity to memorize in the region of seven items (±2). 'Items' are defined by meaning rather than size, so it may be difficult to remember telephone numbers of more than seven digits, but if '01234' is remembered as the 'dialling code' it becomes just one item, and remembering the subsequent numbers '7, 9, 3, 1, 5, 6' becomes simpler. If this sequence of numbers is in turn 'chunked' (or 'associated') as being 'my work phone number' it becomes even easier to remember. This of course assumes that a label for the 'chunk' already exists in long-term memory (LTM). Theoretically, LTM has infinite capacity and lasts for the rest of your life. Tulving (1985) has suggested the useful distinction between three components of LTM:

- There is what is referred to as *semantic* memory that stores concepts and ideas.
- There is also *episodic* (sometimes referred to as 'autobiographical' or narrative') memory that contains memories of events.
- *Procedural* memory concerns skills and 'know-how' rather than 'know-that' knowledge.

People with amnesia, for example, typically lose episodic memory, but other aspects of their memory may be relatively intact. Episodic and semantic memory are more prone to distortion than procedural memory, which is more robust. According to Atherton (2009), a skill lost through lack of practice typically comes back rapidly when called upon, and without significant degradation. However, semantic and episodic memories are more amenable to linguistic description and communication.

Memory involves storing and retrieving data. We can't remember everything which can be frustrating in certain situations (e.g. where did we put that lesson plan that worked so well last year?!). This is because it is impossible to deal with all the information we receive. This can mean that efficient memory relies on forgetting lots of unimportant information, but remembering key facts. As memory is linked to learning this means that it is affected by a number of factors. These include:

- Practice – the more times a piece of information is encountered the more likely it will be committed to LTM.
- Stage theory – information passes through STM on its way to LTM.

- Primacy – the first thing in a list is remembered well.
- Recency/retention – the last thing encountered is remembered well.

---

### Reflective Task 4.2

Is it possible to read the following?
   How can you raed tihs pciee of inofmtoin wehn the wrdos are all jmumbeld up?
   Is teher a paettren?
   Can you sopt it?

### Feedback

When the first and last letters of a word stay the same but the letters in the middle of the word are jumbled up, the brain can still perceive the word that it has learnt, by building up from previous knowledge and LTM.
   This means that memory involves encoding, storage and retrieval but you can't have retrieval unless you go through the process of encoding and storing.

---

# Cognitive pedagogical applications and early years

Cognitive strategies are still teacher led, but learning is far more active for the learners. The learners are more involved in lessons, and they are given tasks, for example problem solving. Gestalt principles are based on recommending that learners should be encouraged to discover the underlying nature of a topic or problem (in other words, the relationship between the component parts). Instruction should be based on the laws of organization, so that there is clear planning with learners in order to organize new learning by connecting it to previous learning.

   The cognitive approach is more of an academic approach based on the principle that learning occurs primarily through exposure to logically presented information. A good analogy that helps in understanding the cognitive approach is to visualize two buckets. Imagine the full bucket of the wise teacher pouring its contents into the empty bucket of the less informed learner. Cognitivism can be understood as being the 'tell' approach to learning so its predominant learning activity is the lecture or didactic teaching approach. Current teaching trends, however, are not always in favour of this approach to teaching and recommend shorter, 'mini-lectures' geared to a 'PlayStation', multi-media culture. The application of teacher-led pedagogy within early years is important, but the amount of didactic teaching being delivered to children needs to take into consideration the concentration levels of the children. Children aged 0–8 can only be 'lectured' to for so long!

*Cognitive techniques used in the classroom*
These include:

- diagrams
- films
- talks by subject specialists
- class presentations
- oral story telling.

Some of the advantages of using a cognitive curriculum or approach include that the curriculum is built on a base of knowledge to extend learners' knowledge or information on concepts and rules. It can provide the rationale upon which the learner can build active learning strategies. This may mean that it is seen as a more rapid learning method than behaviourist or humanist methods of learning.

## Applying cognitive learning to pedagogy in early years

The following guidelines apply if you are applying cognitive learning to early years.

- Information should be presented logically.
- Build from an initial base of information.
- Relationships between 'bits of information' are important.
- The curriculum needs to be organized to reveal its construction.
- As meaning is constructed we need to learn a variety of different information.
- We need to develop children as 'thinkers' if they are to become learners.
- We need to develop strategies and skills in learning to learn effectively.
- Videos, class demonstrations, oral readings and discussions help the learning process.

Like behaviourism, cognitive learning approaches are predominantly teacher led, but the learning process tends to be more active for the children. The children are expected to be more involved in lessons and they are given tasks such as problem-solving activities. These activities are based on the idea that there are thought processes behind behaviour and that changes in behaviour are observed as an indicator of what is going on in the children's minds. Cognitive learning encourages children to discover the underlying nature of a topic or problem (in other words, the relationship) and cognitive pedagogy attempts to build learning around a base of logical organization. For Petty

(2009), cognitivist theorists base their ideas about pedagogy on a belief that education is more than simply communicating facts and procedures to memory. Its main objective is to develop children's independent thinking skills. This is similar to the idea that children can only be 'educated' when they have forgotten what has been learned.

# Humanist pedagogical theory

According to Carl Rogers (1983), the importance of 'teaching' is often overestimated. The key principle according to Rogers is what he refers to as the 'facilitation' of learning. This third approach to learning considered in the chapter, is very different to the behaviourist emphasis that is placed on the environmental factors influencing teaching and learning. Both behaviourist and cognitive approaches to learning adopt something of a scientific approach in terms of the methods they use and the theories that they generate. By contrast the humanist approach can be described as being 'anti-scientific' in the way in which it investigates human beings. The underpinning belief is that we are all unique individuals. Humanism is based on the belief that we are the product of our own particular circumstances. Atkinson et al. (1993) identify that humanism attempts to understand the individual by identifying 'subjective experiences' in order to consider individual thoughts and emotions. Humanist learning theory was developed in America from 1960 onwards and the theory is associated with two psychologists, Carl Rogers and Abraham Maslow. Rogers is associated with 'client-centred learning' and Maslow considers the 'hierarchy' of learning needs. Humanists regard humans as needing to become proactive individuals who are then able to apply 'free will' to their behaviour. Petty (2009) summarizes this approach to understanding humans by emphasizing the importance of making appropriate choices within the learning process. Moreover, the term 'humanist' is generally associated with a variety of approaches that are applied to studying aspects of human behaviour. This provides an holistic approach to studying human behaviour through an emphasis that is placed on the importance of studying the entire person. Humanist theories of learning tend to be value-driven. Although there is an acceptance of a 'natural' desire to learn, there is also an emphasis placed upon empowering learners with a facilitating teacher being of central importance to the learning process.

## Carl Rogers and Malcolm Knowles

Rogers is the founder of person-centred psychotherapy and he has made an important contribution to counselling. Rogers is also associated with the development of humanistic approaches to education. Humanist theories of learning place more of an emphasis on 'what should happen' as opposed to 'what does happen'. The key phrase associated with humanist learning is 'facilitating learning' with teachers being encouraged to empower a situation of self-directed learning. This process results in the teacher needing to take a 'step back' and instead of leading the learning there is an emphasis placed on facilitating learning processes.

Rogers distinguishes two types of learning. There is 'cognitive learning' (academic knowledge such as psychology or multiplication tables) and 'experiential learning' (applied knowledge such as learning about engines in order to repair a car). The key to the distinction is that experiential learning addresses the needs and wants of the learner and is equivalent to personal change and growth. Rogers believes that all human beings have a natural desire to learn so this means that the role of the teacher is to facilitate learning. In helping to facilitate learning, it is important to become aware of the following key aspects of the learning process.

1. Set a positive climate for learning.
2. Clarify the purposes of the learning.
3. Organize and make available appropriate learning resources.
4. Balance the intellectual and emotional components of learning.
5. Share feelings and thoughts with learners without dominating them.

For Rogers, learning is likely to be facilitated when:

1. The student participates completely in the learning process and has control over its nature and direction.
2. The learning process is concerned with practical, social, personal or research interests.
3. Self-evaluation becomes a principal method of assessing progress or success.

Rogers also emphasizes the importance of 'learning to learn' through being open to change. Rogerian learning is therefore based on psychotherapy and humanistic approaches to psychology. It is a profound theory of learning that has influenced pedagogy. Further key ideas include that:

1. Significant learning takes place when the subject matter is relevant to the personal interests of the student.
2. Learning which is threatening to the self (e.g. new attitudes or perspectives) are more easily assimilated when external threats are at a minimum.
3. Learning proceeds faster when the threat to the self is low.
4. Self-initiated learning is the most lasting and pervasive form of learning.

Humanist learning theory applies the ideas of other leading humanist theorists such as Malcolm Knowles and Abraham Maslow. Knowles (1950) attempts to develop a distinctive conceptual basis for pedagogy through consideration of 'self-direction' and on 'group work'. The ideas of Knowles have led to a reconsideration of the concept of 'education' through emphasizing the importance of 'helping learners to learn'. Knowles' learning theory has seven main assumptions linked to motivation.

1. *Learners should acquire as much self-understanding as possible.* The importance of understanding needs, motivations, interests, capacities and goals is emphasized. Learners are encouraged to be viewed in an objective and appropriate way. According to Knowles, the learning process should be based on 'acceptance' and 'respect'.
2. *Learners should develop an attitude of acceptance, and respect towards others.* This is viewed by Knowles as being the attitude on which all human relations depend. Learning is based on distinguishing between human beings and learning concepts. It is regarded as being important to challenge ideas without displaying confrontation. Ideally, this attitude will develop from acceptance, love, and respect, into empathy and the sincere desire to help others.
3. *Learners should develop a dynamic attitude towards life.* There ought to be acceptance of change and the developing awareness that the learning process depends on change. Every experience is visualized as being an opportunity to learn as learning skills develop from this experience.
4. *The learning process depends upon considering the causes, not the symptoms, of behaviour.* Solutions to problems lie in their causes, not in their symptoms. Knowles considers that this aspect of education is a critical component of the learning process.
5. *Learning depends on acquiring the skills necessary to realize individual potential.* Knowles considers that every person has the capability to make a positive contribution to society. Realizing potential requires skills of many kinds. These skills include vocational, social, recreational and artistic attributes. A main purpose of teaching and learning is considered to be enabling individuals to acquire the skills necessary to develop individual potential.

6. *Learners need to ultimately understand the essential values that are central in help-ing to promote a positive learning experience.* They should be familiar with the heritage of knowledge, the great ideas, the great traditions, of the world in which they live. If this idea is applied to early years it is more associated with laying appro-priate foundations for learning. This entails becoming aware of the moral values that bind humans together.

7. *Learners should understand their social circumstances to become ultimately skilful in directing social change.* In a democratic society (i.e. Knowles's ideal), people of all ages participate in making decisions that influence the whole of society. This makes it imperative for basic political, economic and social knowledge to be devel-oped as part of the learning process.

## Applying humanist learning to pedagogy in early years

These humanist principles can be considered any learning activity. At the beginning of any lesson a teacher needs to:

- Establish a climate of equality and mutual respect.
- Determine the expectations of the children.
- Involve the children in planning the objectives of the lesson.
- Acknowledge the value of their learning experiences.

This application of humanistic pedagogy can help in developing key teaching and learning themes.

## Abraham Maslow

Abraham Maslow's (1987) hierarchy of needs is represented in the shape of a pyramid, with the largest and lowest levels of needs at the bottom, and the need for self-actualization at the top. When Maslow's ideas are applied to pedagogy, each component of the hierarchy of needs can be associated with an aspect of pedagogy.

At the base of the pyramid of needs, Maslow refers to the importance of meeting 'physiological' or biological needs if learning is to develop. These physiological needs can be met in early years education in the following ways:

- reduced price and free lunch programmes
- correct room temperatures
- sufficient toilet breaks
- refreshment breaks.

Maslow also makes reference to the importance of ensuring that safety is an essential part of the pedagogical process. In pedagogy in early years this idea can be applied in the following ways:

- Lessons need to be well planned and delivered in a coherent way.
- Classroom behaviour needs to be managed and regulated accordingly.
- Emergency procedures need to be planned, discussed and rehearsed.
- Discipline needs to be applied fairly.
- Expectations need to be reasonable.
- Teacher attitudes ought to be based on being as 'accepting' and non-judgemental as possible.
- Pedagogy ought to be based on giving praise for appropriate responses as opposed to punishing inappropriate responses.

Maslow also emphasizes the importance of engendering feelings of love and belonging within the learning process. With regards to teacher–student relationships, it becomes important for the teacher to develop a number of key aspects of pedagogy. These include the development of:

- Empathetic relationships that are considerate and express interest in individuals.
- Skilled methods of one-on-one instruction.
- Positive comments and constructive feedback.
- Knowledge of children's likes, dislikes and concerns.
- Pastoral and personal skills alongside academic skills.
- Listening skills in order to meet student needs.
- Supportive relationships with students.
- Appropriate assistance for learning support.
- Awareness of students' thoughts, opinions and judgements.
- Trust in children by providing opportunities for responsibility.

With regard to the relationships between children within the class it becomes important to ensure that a number of key pedagogical principles are followed that are based on what Maslow would describe as 'establishing emotional security'. These principles ought to be applied during:

- class meetings
- class discussions
- situations requiring mutual trust
- 'show and tell' and sharing activities.

## Esteem

Humanist learning emphasizes the importance of developing 'self-esteem' within the learning process. A number of key aspects of pedagogy can help in developing learners' self-esteem so that the children become more confident about the learning process in general. It is important to ensure that the development of new knowledge is based on what has been previously learned in order to help ensure the development of the 'scaffolding' process of learning. It is also vital to:

- Focus on the learning strengths of the children and their key learning abilities.
- Take individual needs and abilities into account when planning lessons and carrying them out.
- Teach and model helpful learning strategies for the children (e.g. making sure that you are able to demonstrate what the children are expected to do when they are learning).
- Base new teaching, strategies and plans on manageable learning outcomes.
- Be alert to children's difficulties with the learning process so that you can intervene and help as soon as possible.
- Be available and approachable so that those children having difficulties with learning feel comfortable and are able to 'ask for help'.
- Involve all the children in classroom activities.
- Apply discipline as appropriately as possible.
- Gain respect from others in order to develop a classroom environment where the children are 'positive' as opposed to being 'judgemental'.
- Provide rewards for completing work well.
- Establish a fair system for rewards and punishments.
- Develop and apply a curriculum that enables children to become empathetic and effective listeners:
  ○ Apply cooperative learning in such a way as to develop trust between children
  ○ Involve children in activities that they see as being 'important' and 'worthwhile'.

## Knowledge and understanding

There are a number of key principles that form the basis of developing knowledge and understanding within humanist approaches to learning. The following key principles are of particular importance:

- Allow students time to explore areas of curiosity.
- Deliver teaching sessions that provide an intellectual challenge.
- Plan and prepare lessons that connect areas of learning so that the children are able to compare and contrast ideas.

- Use an interactive approach to pedagogy whenever possible.
- Enable the children to approach topics of learning from as many various angles as possible.
- Provide opportunities for philosophical thought and discussion where appropriate.
- Involve the children in learning activities that challenges their existing knowledge and understanding in an appropriate way.

# Aesthetic learning

Humanist pedagogy places an emphasis on developing the appreciation of human aesthetic qualities. This leads to an emphasis being placed on the following pedagogical aspects of the learning process.

- Classroom materials ought to be arranged in a neat and 'easy on the eye' manner.
- Children's work ought to be displayed regularly if it shows the development and emergence of aesthetic qualities.
- 'Colourful' and 'bright' displays reveal that children are being enabled to apply their aesthetic abilities.
- Learning materials ought to be updated in order to ensure that they do not become 'out of date'.
- Teaching rooms need to be designed so that they create 'varied', 'appealing' and 'interesting' learning areas (e.g. the main teaching room may be painted in colours that 'soften' the atmosphere such as 'light blue').
- Large window areas let in light in order to stimulate learning.
- Well-maintained physical surroundings (clean rooms, keeping walls painted, desks clean and repaired) can help in promoting a positive learning environment.

# Self-actualization

The ultimate goal of humanist learning is for the pedagogical process to enable the children to learn as independently as possible. This is at the heart of the meaning of the important humanist idea of 'self-actualization'. Once learners become 'self-actualized', they are associated with the following attributes:

- The pedagogical process provides children with the freedom to explore learning and discover on their own.
- Learning becomes meaningful and connects 'real life experiences'.
- Teaching sessions enable the children to become involved in projects that help them to develop their powers of self-expression.

Humanists consider humans to be proactive unique individuals who exercise free will over their behaviour. Petty (2009) emphasizes the importance that 'choice' plays in enabling this ability to learn. The argument is developed that choice enables learners to engage with the learning process in an intense, personal way. Humanism emphasizes the importance of drawing on experiences and interaction in order to develop critical thinking, initiative and self-directed learning.

# Learning theories, domains of learning and pedagogy

Table 4.1 shows which teaching and learning strategies are most appropriate for each of the learning theories that we have considered thus far in the chapter.

Table 4.1 provides a guide to some of the learning and teaching strategies that you might choose for your pedagogy. The table shows how pedagogical techniques align with the classical domains of learning. The table shows that

**Table 4.1** Learning domains and learning strategies

| Domain of learning | Humanist | Cognitivist | Behaviourist |
|---|---|---|---|
| Cognitive knowledge | Induction discussion<br>Induction games | Graphic illustrations<br>Interviews and discussions | Tests |
| Transmit information | Discussion<br>Elaboration | Class presentation<br>Reading | Memorizing through<br>association |
| Verify information | Confirmatory<br>discussion | Question and answer<br>Review<br>Test | Question and answer |
| Induce response | Discuss action<br>Visualize action<br>Inductive case study | Lists and steps<br>Demonstration<br>Success stories | Behavioural model<br>Behavioural samples<br>Prompting |
| Strengthen response<br>(practice) | Mental rehearsal | Case study | Worksheets<br>Skill drill (game)<br>Simulation<br>Role play |
| Apply the skill | Action plan<br>Planning guide<br>Elaboration<br>Learning contract | Coaching and feedback | Realistic practice<br>Practical assessment |
| Affective attitude | Self-assessment<br>Encounter and<br>experience<br>Discussion of beliefs<br>Reverse role play<br>Guided reflection<br>Group decision | Authority statement<br>Vicarious experience<br>Debate<br>Testimony | Assessment<br>Pleasant experience<br>Reinforcement |

the cognitivist domain of learning lists the most ways for 'communicating knowledge' whereas the behaviourist domain lists the least. When it comes to 'strengthening skill responses', the behaviourist pedagogical techniques appear to be most useful. Any of the three approaches to pedagogy can be used but what is most interesting appears to be the variable ways that the domains of learning are developed by the three types of pedagogy.

# Learning theories review

The various learning theories have advantages and disadvantages.

## Behaviourist learning

*Key idea.* Learning occurs primarily through the reinforcement of desired responses.

*Pedagogical assumption.* Learning can produce a relatively permanent change in behaviour.

*Key terms.* Behaviour; Conditioning; Reinforcement; Learning Hierarchies.

## Cognitive learning

*Key idea.* Learning occurs primarily through exposure to logically presented information.

*Pedagogical assumption.* Learning is based on the process of constructing new meaning.

*Key terms.* Cognition; Discovery Learning; Insightful Learning; Meaningful Learning.

## Humanist learning

*Key idea.* Learning occurs primarily through reflection on personal experience.

*Pedagogical assumption.* Learning is a process of self-development.

*Key terms.* Self-Actualization; Individual Needs; Intrinsic Motivation.

## Surface and deep learning

A general idea in pedagogical theory is that a learner's conception of what learning is can impact the quality of their learning. This idea is revealed in what is referred to as 'the Jabberwocky exercise'.

## Reflective Task 4.3

Read the passage below and answer the following questions:
Twas brillig, and the slithy toves
Did gyre and gimble in the wabe
All mimsy were the borogoves
And the mome raths outgrabe

Question 1: What were the slithy toves doing in the wabe?
Question 2: How would you describe the state of the borogoves?
Question 3: What can you say about the mome raths?
Question 4: Why were the borogroves mimsy?
Question 5: How effective was the mome raths' strategy?

Most people get the following answers:
Answer to Question 1: Gyring and gambling.
Answer to Question 2: They are all mimsy.
Answer to Question 3. They outgrabe.

### Feedback

Questions 4 and 5 are impossible to answer as it is impossible to fully comprehend the text. The only meaning we are able to find is based on pure speculation. The purpose of the activity is designed to show you that for lower learning (or what is referred to as 'surface learning') we do not require learners to make 'sense of material'. Those tasks which require deeper learning require students to make meanings or 'constructs'. Learning without understanding is called rote learning or surface learning. This means that the learner does not need to make sense of the material in order to get the right answer.

The general idea in pedagogy is that there are are five levels of surface and deep learning. Levels 1–3 are 'surface' learning whereas levels 4 and 5 represent deep learning.

Level 1: Learning leads to an increase in knowledge.
Level 2: Learning leads to 'memorizing' information.
Level 3: Learning is based on acquiring facts or procedures which are to be applied.
Level 4: Learning is based on making sense of concepts. Learners make active attempts to construct 'meaning'.
Level 5: Learning is based on trying to understand 'reality'. Marton and Saljo (1984) summarize this idea when they argue that when you have really learnt something you see things that you couldn't see before. This leads to a completely different view of the world.

Surface learning can be described as 'shallow' or 'superficial' learning as it is based on recalling factual information. In many forms of formal pedagogy in early years, children need to be able to memorize and regurgitate information in order to complete 'memory tests'. As this type of learning involves 'learning by memory', it makes no links to themes or concepts and the learning process is passive. In contrast, deeper learning requires the organization and structuring of information in order to utilize existing knowledge and understanding. This allows learners to form new concepts by challenging existing knowledge.

# Taxonomies of learning

Benjamin Bloom is famous for his identification of what are referred to as key domains of educational activities. These educational activities are:

- *Cognitive*: mental skills (*Knowledge*).
- *Affective*: growth in feelings or emotional areas (*Attitude*).
- *Psychomotor*: manual or physical skills (*Skills*).

Bloom emphasizes the importance that education has in realizing 'mastery' of subjects and the promotion of higher forms of thinking, rather than a simple transferring of facts. Bloom demonstrated that most teaching tends to be focused on 'fact-transfer' and 'information recall'. This is referred to as the lowest level of training as opposed to 'true meaningful personal development' and to this day, this remains a central challenge for teachers and educators.

Bloom's notion of 'taxonomies of learning' links directly back to the concept of 'domains of learning'. The concept can be developed to consider how we can encourage deeper learning in pedagogy through applying the learning taxonomies. The major categories in the psychomotor domain (listed in increasing difficulty – surface to deep learning) are as follows:

1. *Imitation* – observes skill and tries to repeat it.
2. *Manipulation* – performs skill according to instruction rather than observation.
3. *Precision* – reproduces a skill with accuracy, proportion and exactness.
4. *Articulation* – combines one or more skills in sequence with harmony and consistency.
5. *Naturalization* – Completes one or more skills with ease and becomes 'automatic'.

The major categories in the cognitive domain (listed in increasing difficulty – surface to deep learning) include:

1. *Knowledge* – recognition and recall of information.
2. *Comprehension* – interpret, translate or summarize information.

3. *Application* – use information in a situation different from the original learning context.
4. *Analysis* – separates the whole into parts until relationships are clear.
5. *Synthesis* – combines elements to form a new entity from an original one.
6. *Evaluation* – involves acts of decision making or judging based on criteria or a rationale.

The major categories in the affective domain (listed in increasing difficulty – surface to deep learning) include:

1. *Receiving* – being passively aware of certain stimuli, through learning activities such as listening.
2. *Responding* – complying to expectations by creating stimuli that are anticipated.
3. *Valuing* – displaying behaviour consistent with shared beliefs or attitudes.
4. *Organizing* – commitment to 'set values' that are reinforced by behaviour.
5. *Characterizing* – behaviour is completely consistent with internalized values.

At its basic level Bloom's taxonomy provides a simple, quick and easy checklist to help you develop your pedagogical learning outcomes. You can use the increasing difficulty scale to differentiate between your learners offering challenge to some and less challenge to other more needy learners. The more detailed elements within each domain provide additional reference points for learning design and evaluation, whether for a single lesson, session or activity, or for an entire early years syllabus. At its most complex, Bloom's taxonomy can be described as a continuously evolving form of pedagogical theory. At its most practical application, the concepts can lead to the most wonderful and inspiring pedagogy with children in early years.

If we apply Bloom's ideas, we can ensure that we move our pedagogical learning from a 'surface' approach to a 'deeper' understanding and application. A 'deep' approach to pedagogy produces longer lasting learning, and in general deep learners engage with pedagogy more than surface learners. Deep learners structure their understanding of concepts, whereas surface learners tend to just remember unstructured detail. It is generally accepted that deep learners make connections with previous learning whereas surface learners do not have this pedagogical characteristic. Surface learning produces marginally higher scores on tests of factual recall immediately after studying. However, surface learners forget this quickly and as little as a week later, deep learners score higher even in tests of factual recall. Bloom's taxonomy reveals that most learners can adopt both a surface and a deep approach to their learning. Children have been found to make their learning choice in association with the nature of the assessment and the teacher's expectation of learning requirements. This reveals the potential that pedagogy has to develop learners' deep learning skills when these learners arrive with basic surface learning skills.

## Methods to encourage deep learning

There are a number of pedagogical strategies that help to develop 'deep learning'.

1. *Create intrinsic motivation.* Intrinsic motivation is interest in the subject and the tasks in themselves. Try to develop curiosity, interest, passion and 'real-world implications' in your teaching. Try to develop learning activities that are based on creativity, problem solving and individual responses to the pedagogical materials.
2. *Learner activity.* Students need to be 'active' rather than 'passive learners' if they are to enjoy learning. Activities ought to be planned, reflected upon and processed.
3. *Interaction with others.* Group work requires negotiating meaning, expressing and manipulating ideas. Discussion can be used in order to promote high-quality learning.
4. *Establish a good knowledge base.* Without existing concepts it is impossible to make sense of new concepts. It is vital that the children's existing knowledge and experience are brought out in the learning process. The structure of the topic must be made clear so that the learning process can be understood.

## Practical strategies encouraging deep learning

Make sure that your pedagogy is based on 'teaching by asking' as opposed to 'teaching by telling'. Try to adopt the 'pose, pause and pounce' technique when you are asking questions to develop learning. In other words, ask a question and wait for a response before using the response to develop the learning process. The following pedagogical strategy can help in developing deep learning.

1. Think carefully about a clear question and write the question out.
2. Divide the children into groups to work on answering the question.
3. Get feedback from the children.
4. Write up the best ideas.
5. 'Top up' the children's understanding of the key concepts that are being explored.
6. Summarize the main learning goals.

This pedagogical strategy ought to be based on a 'problem-centred approach'. As opposed to teaching 'content', the learners ought to be given a challenge and then be expected to study this content in order to provide a solution to the problem. A way of facilitating this form of pedagogy is to adopt a 'case study approach'. If you give the learners a 'case study' (or scenario) with questions or other tasks to give the topic practical relevance, this can help the children to think 'holistically'. It is also important to ensure that tasks are set in order to develop 'creative responses' from the children. If children are encouraged to design leaflets, and posters, and then in turn enabled to present this content, their sense of deep learning is more likely to be developed.

Try to make sure that you ask 'higher-order questions' from Bloom's taxonomy, as opposed to the lower-order (or 'Jabberwocky') questions. This in turn requires the children to become involved with the 'analysis, synthesis and evaluation' of learning concepts. Make sure that your lessons are structured around 'questions' rather than 'answers', so that curiosity becomes part of the pedagogical process. Questions like 'why do trees lose their leaves in winter?' or 'why is Pascal so lovely?' develop the pedagogical process because your learners are telling you answers as opposed to you telling them the answers! Deep learning involves the critical analysis of new ideas. These ideas ought to be linked to previously known concepts and principles. This in turn helps to develop understanding and long-term retention of concepts so that the learning process can be used for problem solving in unfamiliar contexts. Haughton (2004) outlines that deep learning promotes understanding and allows the learning process to be applied to a variety of contexts. In contrast, surface learning is the tacit acceptance that information is 'isolated' and not connected to a profound level of learning. The learning process becomes characterized by a superficial retention of material and there is no promotion of understanding or long-term retention of knowledge and information.

# Good classroom communication skills

Teaching is generally considered as only 50 per cent knowledge and 50 per cent interpersonal or communication skills. For a teacher in early years, it is not just important to give a quality lesson but it is just as important that the lesson is communicated effectively. Most experienced teachers would agree that communication skills for teachers are just as important as the in-depth knowledge of a particular subject that is being taught.

Teachers need to be aware of the importance of communication skills in teaching. It is also important to realize that children have different levels of skills and needs. The communication skills of the teacher become essential if creative and effective solutions to the challenges within the learning process are to be found. We need effective communication in pedagogy for a variety of reasons. We may need to modify behaviour by using verbal and non-verbal cues in order to get the required behavioural response. To get 'action' from the children or 'persuade' our learners to do a learning activity we may need particularly good communication skills. We need to apply communication skills in order to ensure that our learners understand what they are supposed to be doing. The most common forms of communication are the spoken word, the written word, visual images and body language. Communication can be described as being the process of sending and receiving information. If ever the information does not get to the 'sender/receiver', this can be due to 'distortion'.

## Non-verbal communication

It is not only what you say in the classroom that is important, but it is how you say it that can make the difference to your children. Non-verbal messages are an essential component of communication in the teaching process. Teachers should be aware of non-verbal behaviour in the classroom for three major reasons:

1. Awareness of non-verbal behaviour allows you to become more aware of how your children are communicating.
2. You will become a better communicator if you become aware of non-verbal messages.
3. This mode of communication increases the degree of the perceived psychological closeness between teacher and the learner.

Some major areas of non-verbal behaviours that are important are:

1. *Eye contact*. This is an important channel of interpersonal communication that helps in regulating the flow of communication. It signals interest in others. Eye contact with audiences increases the speakers' credibility. Teachers who make eye

contact open the flow of communication and convey interest, concern, warmth and credibility.

2. *Facial expressions.* Smiling is a powerful cue that transmits happiness, friendliness, warmth, liking and affection. If you smile frequently you will be perceived as being more likeable, friendly, warm and approachable. Smiling is often contagious and students will react favourably and learn more.

3. *Gestures.* If you fail to use gestures while speaking, you may be perceived as being 'unanimated' in your teaching. A lively and animated teaching style captures the children's attention and makes the material more interesting. This can in turn facilitate learning and provide a bit of entertainment. 'Head-nods' can also help in communicating positive reinforcement to the children and indicate that you are listening to what they are saying.

4. *Posture and body orientation.* We communicate numerous messages by the way we walk, talk, stand and sit. Standing erect, but not rigid, and leaning slightly forward communicates to the children that you are approachable, respectful and friendly. Furthermore, interpersonal closeness results when you and your students face each other. Speaking with your back turned or looking at the floor or ceiling should be avoided. This can communicate disinterest to your class.

5. *Proximity.* Cultural norms dictate a comfortable distance for interaction with students. You should look for signals of discomfort caused by invading someone's space. Some of these are signs of discomfort, which include: rocking, leg swinging, tapping and gaze aversion. To counteract this possibility, move around the classroom to increase interaction with your children. Increasing proximity enables you to make better eye contact and increase the opportunities for the children to speak.

6. *Para-linguistics.* This aspect of non-verbal communication includes the vocal elements of tone, pitch, rhythm, timbre, loudness and inflection. For maximum teaching effectiveness, learn to vary these elements of your voice. If you speak to the children in a 'monotone' voice, your style of teaching may be criticized. The children may learn less and then find that they lose interest in learning.

7. *Humour.* This aspect of pedagogy is sometimes overlooked as a teaching tool. Laughter releases stress and tension for both the teacher and the children. It is important to develop an ability to laugh at yourself and encourage your children to make sure that they are never too serious. This in turn fosters a friendly classroom environment that can help in facilitating learning.

8. *Intelligence.* Not everyone can teach well! You need knowledge of your subjects as this will help in engendering confidence. It is also important to ensure that you help in generating an atmosphere that facilitates. To improve your non-verbal skills, you might want to record your speaking on video tape. You could then ask a colleague to suggest how you might change your style of delivery. You might also consider watching a recording of your teaching as this can also help you to evaluate your non-verbal skills.

# Verbal communication

Verbal communication is one way for people to communicate face-to-face. Some of the key components of verbal communication are sound, words, speaking and language. Oral communication is a process whereby information is transferred from a sender to receiver usually by a verbal means but visual aids can also support the process. When you communicate face-to-face, the body language you use alongside the tonality of your voice has a bigger impact than the actual words that you are saying. According to Petty (2009):

- Fifty-five per cent of the impact is determined by your awareness of body language (posture, gesture, eye contact).
- Thirty-eight per cent is determined by the tone of your voice.
- Seven per cent is determined by the content of your words during the communication process.

Therefore, *how you say it* has a major impact on your learners. You have to capture the attention of the audience and make a connection with them. For example, two people saying the same joke, one of them could make the audience laugh due to body language and tone of voice. The second person, however, could use the exact same words but make the audience stare at one another in exasperation.

When you are using oral communication, it is important to make sure that you have visual aids in order to help you to provide more precise information. An electronic teaching board may help to facilitate or enhance the communication process. This aspect of communication can be combined with written words and visual images in order to develop the learning process.

How can we make verbal communication effective?

- Use clear, good pronunciation of words.
- Use simple language that is easy to understand.
- Avoid using jargon, unless it is explained.
- Avoid using abbreviations or acronyms unless they have been previously explained.
- Speak to aid understanding and not to impress.

Effective communication skills in education are easily identified by successful learners. Just as any endeavour will not succeed if the leadership is not effective, so the learning process will be affected negatively if the teacher is not communicating properly. Effective communication in education produces children who understand the information and are in turn motivated to learn more and perform well. When the pedagogical process is based on effective communication, children and teachers become more satisfied with the learning process in general.

In teacher training courses educators often say that the responsibility of the teacher is to communicate in such a way that every child can understand what is happening in the learning process. Although this is true, it must be considered that each child learns differently and at various rates. Communication must be effective in order for learners to succeed, but each child has a different way to process information.

When a teacher communicates effectively, they will be able to have the authority that allows them to avoid confusion and clarify information. Effective communication also gives direction to the learning process. This in turn provides the students with an idea of where they are heading within the pedagogical process. It is when teachers respond to their learners in an effective way that they can in turn communicate knowledge and enthusiasm about their topic. This will in turn generate respect and appreciation of the pedagogical process.

## Summary of key points

In this chapter we have looked at learning theories and their application to education and the classroom. Each learning theory has been discussed in detail showing clear advantages and disadvantages for each strategy. It is hoped you will use the knowledge gained from looking at the learning theories to link to your curriculum and lesson planning. The chapter has also explored how Bloom's 'taxonomies of learning' can be applied to developing learning The contents of the chapter can be used to help develop differentiated learning outcomes that will challenge your more able learners as well as meeting the needs of your less able learners. The final section of the chapter has explored the importance of communication skills. The chapter content emphasizes that non-verbal communication skills are just as important as verbal skills. Teaching is not an impossible profession. It can be argued that teaching, just like learning is a discipline. This means that it is important to learn from teaching experiences. Reflect on these experiences. Retain what is positive. Amend and adapt what has been less than positive. This is essentially at the centre of the craft of teaching.

## Self-assessment questions

Complete the following sentences:

1. Learning is a relatively permanent change in ............................?
2. How does advertising work?
3. Who has used operant conditioning on you and what did they get you to do?
4. Behaviourists believe that all behaviour is ............................?
5. Name a major cognitivist theorist?
6. Name a humanist theorist who has been discussed within this chapter?
7. What is surface learning?
8. State three ways to apply deeper learning strategies in the classroom.

## Moving on feature

This chapter has introduced learning theories which feature in every aspect of your planning and presentation of teaching. These theories also impact upon how you manage your classroom. The chapter also focuses on the use of surface and deeper learning which you should consider when writing learning outcomes and planning activities for learners. Continue to think about positive communication skills when studying classroom management as you need to develop your own skills and those of your learners.

## Further reading

Petty, G. (2009), *Teaching Today* (4th edn). Cheltenham: Nelson Thornes.

An excellent textbook that is written in an accessible way and makes clear links to applying theory to practice.

# 5 Enhancing Learning and Early Childhood Studies

## Learing outcomes

After reading this chapter you should be able to:

- define the terms 'widening participation', 'curriculum', 'inclusion' and 'inclusive practice' within the parameters of learning and teaching in early years;
- understand and evaluate some of the ways that the curriculum can be developed to promote inclusive practice;
- critically appraise the scope and potential limitations of developing the curriculum to promote inclusive practices within early years.

# Introduction

This chapter considers key factors that enhance learning and teaching in early years. Awareness of the importance of developing the 'curriculum', through 'widening participation', 'inclusion' and 'inclusive practice' are important aspects of promoting best practice for learning and teaching in early years. The chapter content aims at:

- Identifying defining characteristics of the curriculum and inclusive practice.
- Exploring issues associated with widening participation and inclusion.
- Exploring some of the dilemmas that may occur for teachers in early years who plan, design, implement and review a curriculum that supports inclusive practice.

The overarching aim of the chapter is to assist you in identifying best practice in teaching in early years so that you will enhance the learning of the children you are likely to work with. Throughout the chapter there are formative activities that reinforce learning. These activities encourage you to reflect on developing the curriculum in order to facilitate inclusive practice in early years. The chapter explores a range of key issues for teachers in early years. Some of these key issues revolve around:

- Defining the 'curriculum' by considering 'widening participation', 'inclusion' and 'inclusive practices' and their relationship to 'curriculum development' for inclusive practice.
- Implementing, reviewing, evaluating and adapting the curriculum in order to promote inclusive practice.
- Equality, diversity and the ethical/legal issues that are associated with pedagogy.

# Defining the curriculum, widening participation and inclusion

## Reflective Task 5.1

What is your understanding of the terms 'curriculum', 'widening participation' and 'inclusion'?

⇨

> **Feedback**
>
> This part of the chapter will focus upon defining these key terms and their use within educational contexts. The chapter will then go on to explore the influences of these terms on the development, delivery and review of an inclusive curriculum.

The *Oxford English Dictionary* (*OED*) defines the curriculum in the following way: *A course; specifically, a regular course of study or training, as at school or university.* Kelly (2004, p. 5) defines the term curriculum as: *All the learning which is planned and guided, whether carried on in groups or individually.* In simplistic terms, the curriculum can therefore be defined as a course of planned or guided learning completed on an individual basis or in groups.

An excellent example of a curriculum currently in use in early years in the United Kingdom is the Early Years Foundation Stage (EYFS). This is a curriculum framework for planning programmes of learning for children aged from 0 to 5 years. The EYFS is based on 4 main themes and 16 standards. The four main themes are a 'unique child'; 'positive relationships'; 'enabling environments' and 'learning and development'. These EYFS learning themes support the UK primary school learning goals of 'communication, language and literacy'; 'personal social and emotional development'; 'problem solving and reasoning'; 'creative development'; 'physical development' and 'knowledge and understanding of the world'.

'Widening participation' in education has been an important part of education in early years for a number of years. The widening participation agenda is concerned with ensuring that education is not restricted to a few privileged groups of society. In summary, widening participation can be considered to be an aspect of inclusion that considers not so much how children can be included in learning activities 'in the classroom' but more fundamentally 'who' should be included in participating in learning (or the curriculum) and why. By widening participation to as many children as possible an attempt is being made to ensure that a diverse range of children are being educated in early years. Ideally this diversity will include a range of children of differing needs who are included within the curriculum. The widening participation agenda in education in early years in the United Kingdom has gathered momentum since 1997 with the election to power of New Labour. As opposed to being concerned with traditional learners, attempts were made to include children with special educational needs within mainstream education. This aspect of widening participation has led to a transformation of learning and teaching in early years in the United Kingdom.

How is the term 'inclusion' defined? The *OED* online provides a useful definition of inclusion, which is: *The act of including or the state of being included.* This implies that inclusion is primarily about positioning a learner with particular needs in a mainstream class so that they are included in that learning situation. The act of inclusion also suggests some activity, or 'action' to ensure that inclusion can take place. Inclusion may lead to the removal of physical barriers that prevent access, for example, providing a ramp for children who are wheelchair users to access a school. Inclusion may also lead to the provision of funds to learners from socially disadvantaged backgrounds so that they attend specialist programmes of learning. Some of these actions may encourage widening participation and inclusion, in terms of physical, financial, and to some extent religious barrier removal, but how far do these activities support 'inclusion' in terms of equality of opportunity to access learning in the classroom or 'inclusive practice'? The following section of this chapter will explore this theme in detail.

# Curriculum design and implementation for inclusive practice

## Reflective Task 5.2

By now you will be familiar with the concept of planning a curriculum for delivery and you will have highlighted some of the constraints and issues around this. What you may not have done is thought in-depth about some of the more specific needs that individual children may have within these groups. Take some time to reflect on what these needs might be when planning a curriculum for the following groups of children in order to promote inclusion and make a note of how their particular needs may impact further upon your planning:

- children aged 4–6 with English as an 'additional language';
- children aged 7–8 with special educational needs;
- children aged 5–8 with autism.

> **Feedback**
>
> Tomlinson (1997) defines inclusive learning as *the greatest degree of match or fit between how learners learn best, what they need and want to learn, and what is required of the sector, a college and teachers for successful learning to take place* (Gravells and Simpson, 2009, p. 34). For Tummons (2009, p. 94), 'inclusive practice' is: *thinking about our teaching, and our curricula, in such a way that any student can access it to the best of their potential ability*. Petty (2009) discusses differentiation along similar lines and defines it as: *adopting strategies that ensure success in learning for all, by accommodating individual differences of any kind*. This interest in inclusive learning is based on a fundamental theme that in order to provide the best opportunities for learning to take place we must be flexible and adapt our teaching practices accordingly. In summary, 'inclusive practice' can be defined as 'the use of a variety of differentiated approaches to teaching and learning in the classroom in order to deliver the curricula content in such a way as to promote a wider access to learning for as many learners as possible.'

If we consider the previous definitions of inclusive practice and think further about their implications for curriculum development, a key related area for consideration is differentiation. You will often find inclusion and differentiation discussed together because inclusive learning links to differentiated teaching and learning practices. So what is a differentiated classroom? This has been described by Tomlinson (2001, p. 1) as a classroom which: *provides different avenues to acquiring content, to processing or making sense of ideas and to developing products so that each student can learn effectively.* Tomlinson (1997) then goes on to discuss the advantages of a differentiated classroom as it provides the best access to learning, promotes effectiveness of learning and encourages motivation in learning. Tomlinson's (1997) notion of a differentiated classroom emphasizes that learning experiences need to be based upon readiness to learn, learning interests and learning profiles. This means that the content and activities in the session and the expected learning outcomes are developed according to the varied needs of the group and the individual learners. The consequences are that teaching and learning activities are focused on key concepts of learning so that teachers and students work together to ensure that learners are challenged and continually engaged in learning. Some of Tomlinson's (1997) teaching and learning strategies to promote a differentiated learning experience for the learners are summarized as follows:

- The teacher should combine time and space with effective learning activities.
- There should be flexible grouping which ensures fluidity of working arrangements that are consistent as far as possible.
- This should include a range of strategies such as whole class learning, paired learning, small group learning, teacher selected learning groups and random learning groups.
- Flexible use of time is needed to respond to the learners' needs at any given time.
- A wide variety of classroom management strategies are needed such as independent study, interest groups, learning buddies and tiered assignments in order to help to target instruction to the students' needs.

There should be clear criteria for success developed at both group and individual levels to provide guidance to the children as to what would be a successful learning outcome.

Formative and summative assessment activities should be varied in order to enable the learners to demonstrate their own thoughts and develop their learning. These broader but important factors provide some theoretical parameters which guide the more practical aspects of planning for teaching and learning. This means that developing schemes of work and planning delivery are critical aspects of the curriculum process. As you will be aware by now, the fundamental areas for consideration when planning a scheme of work include:

- the learning content and overall aims of the curriculum;
- the time constraints which the teacher has to work within;
- the best opportunities for learning and how learning is to be delivered;
- the type of knowledge and skills to be developed;
- the requirements of national standards and targets;
- the methods to be adopted in order to measure to what extent learning has taken place;
- any specialist knowledge that is required to deliver the curriculum;
- the available physical and human resources that must be considered in the planning.

The scheme of work is the framework document that is developed by teachers to help them to identify what is to be included in each individual session plan. Good session plans will include the relevant information from a scheme of work but will also be expanded to provide more detail of how particular sessions will be delivered. This may be the most appropriate point for teachers to consider the more specific detail and information that is required to deliver a truly inclusive curriculum. These may include, for example, specific details about the entry behaviour and the individual needs of each learner, for example levels of ability in literacy and numeracy.

All teachers need to think about how to make the curriculum accessible. It is important to consider all of the above recommendations and then move on one step further to think about the needs of your learners as individuals and how the curriculum can be planned to be as inclusive as possible. As we have discussed earlier in the chapter, a truly inclusive curriculum takes account of the needs of the learners in order for them to be provided with the best opportunities to learn.

According to Gravells and Simpson (2009) student teachers should be proactive at the planning stage in thinking about the wider implications for meeting the individual needs of the learners. This means that it is important to consider:

- Whether the physical learning environment provides any barriers to accessibility for learners and what can be done to address this.
- Differentiated teaching and learning activities planned at both scheme of work and session planning level to ensure that all of the learners can access learning equally.
- Making reference to a variety of cultures, religions and traditions.
- The diversity of your students.

As teachers, our primary concern should always be that we are enabling our learners to fulfil their full potential by providing them with the most appropriate learning opportunities possible. As indicated earlier in this chapter, children with special educational needs are often included within mainstream schools as opposed to being educated separately in isolated institutions. This requires teachers to become aware of the importance of meeting diverse needs within learning and teaching in early years.

Although this indicates the relative success of the widening participation agenda the very fact that early years settings are recruiting learners from such diverse backgrounds brings a range of educational challenges that the teacher will have to consider when planning a curriculum that can be delivered in a truly inclusive way.

Let us consider a variety of groups of children in early years and by considering their needs and how this might provide challenges for teachers planning a curriculum to ensure inclusive practice.

# Children aged 4–6 years with English as an additional language

Children aged 4–6 years with English as an additional language can have a number of educational needs. The children may struggle with the academic curriculum as the UK curriculum is often based on targets and meeting standards. A more practical curriculum may be more appropriate to the children's learning style, individual motivations and needs. If these learners demonstrate challenging forms of behaviour like refusing to participate in tasks and being 'withdrawn' you will have to develop strategies and approaches to cope with this situation. This may include planning individual tasks for these children or adapting the curriculum to enable it to meet the needs of the children more effectively. This range of strategies, some of which do not directly relate to the curriculum itself may encourage and enable the children to access the curriculum and gain as much as possible from the learning process.

Mainstream primary school children (aged 0–8) may appear to be a discrete group of learners but it is important to realize the importance of encouraging differentiated approaches to learning and teaching for children who have English as an additional language. A good rule of professional practice is to ensure that a range of curriculum development strategies are considered for all of your learners. One of these strategies that may be considered is reflecting on the range of different learning styles that will be present in a classroom at any one time. There has been research carried out on learning styles, such as with the Visual, Auditory Kinaesthetic Module (VAK) that was developed by Fernald, Keller, Orton, Gillingham, Stillman and Montessori in the 1920s. The main thrust of this research is that learners need to be enabled to complete learning tasks in a way which best suits their needs. This means that some learners may be more visual and learn best from the use of visual diagrams rather than linear lists. Other learners prefer to complete practical activities in order to learn and others may learn best by hearing something, and then reciting the information. This research has summarized that learners will not necessarily fall neatly into one category, and that learners are more likely to have a combination of preferred learning approaches, such as visual/kinaesthetic, or auditory/visual. More recently Howard Gardner's (1993) 'multiple intelligences' categorize learners as having particular 'intelligences'. Gardner proposes that a learner may be 'verbal/linguistic' or 'musical/rhythmic' or 'mathematical' so that teachers should adapt their teaching and learning approaches to meet these various needs. The work of Gardner has been criticized, with other educationalists such as Frank Coffield (2004) concluding that in general it is good teaching practice to use a range of teaching and learning strategies, and that if this is done effectively all the learners in the group will be able to access the curriculum. Coffield (2004) does however dispute the idea that there are eight forms of intelligence and asks 'Why 8? Why not 9 or more?'

What other considerations need to be made in order to facilitate as inclusive a curriculum as possible? If, for example, you are using an electronic teaching board how are you going to include those children with special educational needs? What about tactile learners, what about learners who learn best from social interaction and group work? Vygotsky (1978) argues that learning is a social activity and that social interaction plays a fundamental role in the development of cognition. The argument has been developed to propose that for meaningful learning to take place, social interaction is necessary. A more didactic approach to teaching where you are delivering content via an electronic board can mean that the children are not fully engaged in the learning process. One might even argue that this means that an inclusive curriculum for all learners is not being provided. This is without considering the implications for learners in the session who may have hidden disabilities (see later in this chapter for detailed discussion of legal issues around this area). The general rule is that it is important to ensure that your teaching is characterized by the presence of a variety of pedagogical approaches in order to enhance the classroom experience for all the children.

## Children aged 7–8 with special educational needs

This group of learners may find that they face many challenges integrating into formal learning and teaching within primary schools. The social and environmental barriers faced by these children can mean that teachers face many challenges facilitating learning with these children. As a result of the needs of these learners there are a number of considerations that ought to be made in respect of learning and inclusive practice. These considerations can depend on whether or not the children are expected to follow the formal national curriculum. In Chapter 4 of this book we made reference to the ideas of Malcolm Knowles (1989) (cited in Tennant, 1997). This theory of learning relies on a range of assumptions about the learning process. A key assumption is that the best form of learning is when learners become self-directed, and motivated so that there is an autonomy over the learning process. This approach is adopted in order to ensure that the learners become interested in the curriculum. This particular approach to learning emphasizes the importance of 'social skills' within the learning process and their relation to 'motivation'. Motivation can be regarded as being potentially intrinsic or extrinsic to the learning process. Whether motivation is intrinsic or extrinsic in orientation can have an impact upon the success or otherwise of the curriculum. *Generally, intrinsic interest in a subject is typically associated with high levels of intrinsic motivation and this in turn is linked to successful learning/achievement outcomes* (Brown et al., 1998, p. 16). Extrinsic motivation is associated with factors outside or external to the individual. Brown et al. (1998, p. 16) explains that *learners who are extrinsically motivated are influenced by external rewards and pressures. Learners who have high extrinsically motivating factors can feel 'controlled' by them and this can have a negative impact on their intrinsic motivation.* Educationally, intrinsic motivation (or intrinsic interest in the subject) is seen as being the most desirable type of motivation to promote learning as it leads to 'deep learning' approaches and learning outcomes that are: 'concerned with conceptual understanding of the material, and incorporating this into one's existing knowledge' (Fry et al., 2003, p. 65). However, it is generally acknowledged that learners who have strong extrinsically motivating factors will still do what is necessary to 'please the teacher'. This form of 'strategic learning' may not always lead to deep learning, so if we consider children aged 7–8 years with special educational needs, how can we develop a curriculum that is inclusive and provides the best opportunities and motivation for learning?

It may be worth developing individual learning plans for these children and including SMART targets for learning (Specific, Measurable, Achievable, Relevant and Time-bound). It is so important however, to consider individual needs, abilities, preferred ways of learning, appropriate learning targets and preferred methods of assessment. It may be that individual learning plans are reviewed on a one-to-one basis with the tutor. This type of approach to providing an inclusive curriculum can be considered to be one of the best approaches for enhancing learning as it is a means of responding to the individual needs of the children. As opposed to focusing on national targets and a national curriculum, this approach to enhancing learning attempts to adapt the curriculum according to the individual needs of the children. If this way of enhancing learning is characterized by structuring and planning within the learning process it in turn becomes possible to develop strategies for measuring the learning that has taken place with children aged 7–8 with special educational needs.

Children who combine practical and academic learning tasks in the classroom have an opportunity to access a more vocational curriculum. This can mean that they have the opportunity to develop more of a variety of skills. The curriculum planned for this group of children is likely to require thought and consideration. There are a tremendous range of special educational needs so it is important to ensure that the individual needs of the children are met. When planning an inclusive programme for these children, it is important to make sure that there is an appropriate balance of knowledge, skills and practical development for each learner.

Lave's (1990) theory of situated learning is one which may be appropriate to consider when thinking about designing an inclusive curriculum for these children. Lave theorizes that learning, as it normally occurs, is a function of the activity, context and culture in which it occurs – it is 'situated'. This contrasts with much classroom learning which involves knowledge that is abstract and out of context. The principles of situated learning are based on the idea that social interaction is a critical component of the learning process and that knowledge needs to be presented in an authentic context. Lave is saying that learning in context and in 'real' situations is the most desirable way of promoting inclusion in the learning process. When this occurs Lave believes that learners then become part of a 'community of practice' which embodies certain beliefs and behaviours to be acquired and that as the new learner moves from the periphery of the community to its centre, he/she becomes more active or engaged within the culture and eventually assumes the role of 'expert'. Lave and Wenger (1990) call this the process of legitimate peripheral participation. The use of situated learning and communities of practice may benefit learners in a group. They make learning 'real' and 'meaningful' in order to support the development of practical vocational skills in the workplace. This is further supported by the use of subject specialists who are able to deliver the academic content of a programme such as this and link it effectively to work practice.

## Children aged 5–8 with autism

All children can encounter problems with their learning, whether they are considered to have a learning difficulty or disability or not. However, there may be additional challenges for children with autism. Autism is a neurological condition that influences the cognitive thinking of the individual. There are varying degrees of severity with autism. Mild autism may require less specialist curriculum planning and children aged 5–8 with this form of autism may be able to complete many of the learning goals of the formal curriculum. Less mild versions of autism can lead to children becoming isolated and detached from the formal curriculum. In order to enhance the learning of these children it is essential to meet their individual needs and then adapt the curriculum accordingly.

Tummons (2009, p. 101) argues that *the social model of disability puts its focus not on an individual, and thereby on any physical or mental disability that the person might have but on the society within which they live.* He goes on to say that: *Under the social model of disability, the emphasis is on changing the world around us so that we can all participate.* In summary, in any learning situation, the emphasis is on adapting the environment and redesigning teaching and learning activities in order to promote access to learning for all children. This opposes the view of seeing the learning difficulty as a barrier to learning itself. In reality, this may not always be easy, but a good teacher will always strive to provide equality of opportunity for all children in the school.

This chapter is primarily focused upon curriculum development in order to enhance learning so measuring the progress made by the learners becomes important. The assessment of learning becomes a key way of measuring the progress that is being made by the children. Ideally the curriculum will have been inclusive in order to ensure that the children's learning has been as successful as possible. The following case study reveals the extent of planning that may be required if you are to enhance the learning of children aged 5–7 who have study skills needs.

## Case study

Sabina is planning her curriculum delivery for a group of children that she is going to teach after they have previously been taught by an experienced teacher. The class she is taking over has a number of children aged 5–7 with basic study skills needs. Sabina is in her second teacher training placement and has some experience of teaching groups of children who have special educational needs. Sabina has specialized in English and she enjoys teaching children aged 5–7 reading and writing skills. In her planning she regularly considers adopting differentiated approaches in order to promote inclusive practice as Sabina realizes that this is an effective way of meeting the individual needs of the children. Sabina uses a variety of teaching methods with the children and she is also very interested in different formative assessment methods. When she meets with the teacher she is replacing, Sabina finds that the style of teaching preparation she has been used to will need to be employed with this group of learners because of the vastly different levels of ability being shown by the children. In order to ensure inclusivity and to meet the wider needs of the children, the learning and teaching resources need reviewing in respect of the individual needs of the children. Sabina realizes that she will need to spend a tremendous amount of time developing session plans for the children in the group as individual learner needs will have to be considered in detail. This will require that detailed individual learning outcomes will need to be set. Individualized resources will have to be identified and individual approaches to assessment (methods and resources for measuring learning) will also need to be considered.

---

### Practical task

Select two groups of children that you are currently working with who have very different needs. Choose one of your lesson plans and evaluate the content in terms of how effective the session promotes inclusive practice. It may help if you consider the following questions. Can you identify where you have planned individual learning outcomes to meet the children's needs? Can you identify where you have planned individualized approaches (strategies) to teaching and learning? Have you identified specific assessment strategies that are appropriate to the learners' needs and abilities and devised/located resources that are appropriate both for supporting learning and measuring learning (assessment) in a fair, equitable and accessible way?

---

# Reviewing, evaluating and adapting the early years curriculum to promote inclusive practice

---

### Reflective Task 5.3

Think about a group of children you have recently taught. Ask yourself the following questions:

⇨

- Do you think you delivered a truly inclusive curriculum?
- If not, what issues were there with the curriculum delivery that you can identify and how do you know that there were inclusion issues; in other words, on what evidence do you base this judgement on? If the curriculum 'worked well' and promoted inclusion, why did this happen?
- List three things that you would change if you had the opportunity to deliver this curriculum again to promote as much inclusive practice as possible?
- What constraints can you identify that may prevent you from implementing all the changes that you might wish?

## Feedback

As a teacher you will always be striving to improve your professional practice and one of the ways that you can do this is by evaluating and reflecting on the lessons you have delivered in order to review how successful the delivery was and how any future teaching can be improved.

Tummons (2009) provides some examples of trainee teachers' responses to the question, what is evaluation? These examples include *finding out if your curriculum did what it set out to do; judging fitness for purpose; seeing if the resources you use are at an appropriate standard; making sure the learners get what they expect to get, and what everyone else expected they'd get.* Considering this information helps you to identify ways of enhancing learning in early years.

This is a brief list, but it does provide a starting point to discuss the concept and process of evaluating curriculum delivery with regard to inclusive practice. What are the best ways of gathering information about the success of the curriculum you are delivering?

A traditional method of finding out whether or not the curriculum is working is through 'action research'. This type of research is discussed in the next chapter. It is characterized by finding out information about the curriculum, recommending improvements and in turn assessing the effectiveness of these improvements. Questionnaires are often used as a means of gathering feedback from other teachers about what is working well and what needs modifying or adapting. There are however, a number of challenges in obtaining what may be referred to as valid information. One of these issues is phrased as 'questionnaire fatigue'. At the end of a busy day teaching, the teachers you are keen to consult with may be reluctant to take part in this process even though the information may provide a useful way of analysing the curriculum in order to help learning experiences in the future. Questionnaires may also be less than 'user-friendly' as they can be difficult to understand and complete. It may be difficult enough to get staff to complete questionnaires about the learning process but imagine how challenging this process may be with parents and children. Moreover, with children there is the added complication of needing to ensure that ethical procedures have been followed. In summary, questionnaires may be useful in providing some information about the success of the curriculum delivery, but as professional teachers we should be looking at complementary quantitative and qualitative ways of evaluating the curriculum in order to improve the future experiences of our students.

The curriculum may be measured in quantitative ways by looking at the 'success' and failure statistics of the curriculum. If a school has good attendance and the children meet the curriculum targets, we may assume that all is well with the curriculum delivery. If, however, large numbers of children are absent and the children appear to be missing the targets set by the national curriculum, there may be issues with the way the curriculum has been designed and delivered. These complex issues may not be picked up by the process of a tick box questionnaire.

In order to make an informed decision regarding future actions or changes to curriculum delivery, questionnaire data can be useful but it is always important to give a detailed analysis of what is impacting upon learning and teaching experiences. One of the most effective ways of gathering information from children about what they enjoy learning is by meeting with them and talking about their experiences. Teaching is a profession that depends on successful communication. By talking to the children and finding out what is working well or otherwise and then adapting the curriculum accordingly, it becomes possible to enhance learning. This process can allow the children and the staff to shape the curriculum by identifying the issues with respect to curriculum design and delivery. The meetings can be vital in helping a teaching team to plan for the future improved delivery of the curriculum. The outcomes of meetings such as this can then be formalized and put into effect for the future benefit of the curriculum.

Another important way of evaluating the success or otherwise of the curriculum is by looking at the learning journey of children learners. Have the children achieved what they set out to do? If they have, why? Did you adapt your teaching strategies and the resources used to enable the children to have full access to the curriculum? Did you provide alternative assessment methods? Did you ensure that the children were provided with effective pastoral support as and when they needed it? Conversely, if you have children who have not progressed as they would have wished what are the reasons for this? Did you plan and deliver the curriculum in a way that is inclusive for the children? Did you consider them as individuals within a group when you were doing your session planning? Are the issues with progression to do with factors outside the curriculum delivery itself, such as poor attendance, or personal problems that have impinged upon learning? Have you failed to meet individual learner needs by not adapting your teaching approaches to support each learner's learning and progression? All of these questions can help you to consider ways of enhancing learning through the curriculum.

In order to evaluate the progress of groups of children and individual learners and to plan for improved future practices it may be useful to use a framework for reflection that will help you to focus upon key issues and what can be done to address them. A recognized model of reflective practice that can be particularly useful is Brookfield's (1985) notion of 'critical lenses'. According to Brookfield there are four critical lenses for reflecting on practice. These 'lenses' are:

- our own perspective;
- the point of view of our learners;
- the point of view of our colleagues;
- reflection on pedagogical theory.

Using Brookfield's critical lenses is a useful and practical framework that can be used by teachers in early years to evaluate information and produce an action plan for change based upon that information. Consider the following case study.

## Case study

Peter is completing a review of his teaching as part of his professional development. Peter asks his colleagues for their views on what he is doing 'well' and 'less well' in respect of his teaching. Peter also requests that the staff consider how the children respond to him when he is being given this feedback. Although generally, the information he receives is positive, there are one or two areas of development that have been raised that need some careful consideration. Peter's teaching mentor has identified that some of the resources Peter is using could be improved. Peter is also told by a colleague that the teaching and learning methods he uses could be more creative. Peter is aware that there is a forthcoming opportunity for professional development and he decides to try and find out how he can develop his teaching practice via this professional development. Some of the staff who are teaching on the programme have attended a staff development workshop on 'story telling for children aged 5–7 years'. Peter decides that this is an area of professional development that he needs to work on following this feedback about his teaching. At the same time, Peter decides that he needs to become more aware of the needs that are associated with dyslexia and he identifies that he needs to do more research into the subject to increase his knowledge. Upon reflecting on these two activities, Peter considers that he is in a position to develop as a teacher in respect of meeting the needs of the children he teaches. In going through this process of reviewing professional development needs, Peter has applied Brookfield's critical lenses to reflect on and evaluate his own practice. Hopefully this will enable Peter to meet the needs of the children in the future.

### Practical task

Evaluate the process that Peter has gone through in terms of Brookfield's critical lenses. When you are next provided with the opportunity to evaluate your practice apply Brookfield's critical lenses as a way of helping you to develop your reflective practice.

# Equality and diversity – ethical and legal issues and curriculum development for inclusive practice

## Practical task

Locate your organization's Equal Opportunities Policy, this may be available from your main office and may also be referred to on your organization's website? Read it through and note how many references are made to legislation and 'Acts of Law'.

### Feedback

As a teacher it is important that you are aware of the legislation surrounding your profession and the implications for your teaching practice if you are to enhance learning. It is also important to be aware of the legislation that exists to protect the children you are teaching. This section of the chapter provides an overview of some of the key areas of legislation you need to be aware of when you are attempting to develop the curriculum in order to enhance inclusive practice. The following content discusses some of the issues that are associated with stereotyping individuals, alongside considering gender, ethnicity and cultural issues.

The Disability Discrimination Act (DDA) was passed in 1995, was extended in 2002 and amended in 2005. The original legislation was passed to protect disabled people from discrimination and defined disability as follows: *a person has a disability if he or she has a physical or mental impairment, which has a substantial and long-term adverse effect on his/her ability to carry out normal day to day activities.*

In 2001, the Special Educational Needs and Disability Act (2001) also known as SENDA (part 4 of the DDA) brought education into the remit of the DDA. This extension, which was implemented in September 2002, ensures that disabled learners are not treated less favourably than other learners. The Act uses a broader spectrum in defining disability as the legislation refers to: *people with physical or sensory impairments, dyslexia, medical conditions, mental health difficulties and learning difficulties.*

The 2002 extension to the Act is particularly important for those in the teaching profession as it relates directly to educational organizations. It is important for teachers in schools to *anticipate* the needs of children with disabilities as opposed to *responding* to the needs of children in their educational context.

As a result of this legislation it is deemed as being desirable that educational organizations have in place the mechanisms to encourage the disclosure of disabilities. The ideal aim is for adjustments to be made prior to learners joining the programme. This may be done via the recruitment and interview process. Following the 2002 extension to the Act, many organizations offering educational programmes reviewed their recruitment and interview procedures. These reviews were completed in order to encourage applicants to disclose disabilities that could impact upon their educational progress prior to joining educational programmes. However, according to Tummons (2009, p. 100) it is important to bear in mind that learners *are not obliged to tell anyone they have a disability* and that *it is possible for a learner with a disability to feel that they have been discriminated against even if they have not revealed the disability.*

Tummons (2009) goes on to indicate that the legislation is there to provide a framework for teachers to work within and that this framework should be liberating and not oppressive. At all times it is important not to lose sight of the concept of 'reasonableness' when adapting buildings or practice. Tummons (2009, p. 100) indicates some areas of practice where adjustments should be made such as *adjustments to the exterior of buildings, to course materials, to assessment practices and to classrooms and workshops.* Tummons also emphasizes that trainee teachers should not feel isolated when they are planning a curriculum of inclusivity. It is important to ensure that all available support mechanisms are used, such as seeking specialist advice from learning difficulty and disability coordinators. Other sources of support may include practice mentors, other more experienced teachers, awarding bodies and external support networks such as action groups for the disabled. The learners themselves should always be at the centre of the process and where possible, guidance from them as to meeting their needs should be sought. Some of the implications of including children in early years in the learning process are considered in the following case study.

## Case study

Robert, is a trainee teacher, and he has been working with children aged 6–8 years who have a number of learning difficulties and disabilities. One of the children that Robert has been working with ('Sophie') is visually impaired. Sophie's parents have asked for learning materials to be provided that meet her needs. Sophie's reading materials need to be enlarged by 20 per cent; Sophie also needs to be at the front of the classroom in order to follow learning activities on the interactive board. Sophie's parents have also requested that the teacher faces the front of the class when delivering didactic content in order to enable her to engage more fully with the teacher's delivery of the teaching content. It was also agreed that Sophie will be accompanied by a teaching assistant during teaching. This teaching assistant will help Sophie to participate in the learning process in order to take care of her pastoral needs. Robert is keen to support Sophie but he is unsure about his ability to realize this aim. Robert decides to arrange to meet with Sophie's parents in order to discuss ways of improving the educational experience. Robert also plans to meet with his professional mentor, who is an experienced teacher in order to ask for assistance and guidance at regular intervals during his delivery of the programme. This is in order to discuss practical advice in ensuring that Sophie is fully included in the learning process. Robert is aware that meeting Sophie's needs will at times mean extra preparation work for him, but he is keen to support Sophie's progress as much as possible.

---

### Practical task

When you are planning the teaching for your next class take time to consider where you have made 'reasonable adjustments' in your planning to accommodate the needs of your children. How will this manifest itself in practice when you are delivering the session and what additional work, if any, does this lead to when preparing and delivering the session itself?

There are a range of additional issues to consider when thinking about equality and diversity and enhancing learning through an inclusive curriculum. Some of these issues include considering the impressions of the learners and the teacher, the dangers of stereotyping, gender issues, cultural considerations and consideration of ethnicity.

In terms of curriculum development for inclusive practice it is the teacher's job to remove as many barriers to learning as possible. According to Petty (2009) the first impressions formed from both the teachers and learners' sides can have a lasting influence on the development of any relationship as these first impressions can be difficult to overcome. Petty goes on to argue that when we meet a person for the first time, we subconsciously select information that we process in order to characterize a person. Petty (2009, p. 77) states that these characterizations are based upon factors such as: *Dress, hairstyle, facial expressions, posture, gestures, age, ethnic origins, gender, as well as what the person says, or how they say it.* This occurs so that we can best evaluate how to deal with or approach someone for the first time. Petty (2009, p. 79) defines stereotyping as: *the tendency to attribute, to an individual, traits that we assume are characteristics of the group to which we believe they belong. This of course tends to blind the perceiver to the differences between the members of a group.*

As a teacher it is important to ensure that we design the curriculum to be inclusive but also that the learners feel that they are positively and equally valued when participating in the learning process. As trainee teachers it is unlikely that you will set out to provide unequal opportunities for your learners, but, according to Petty (2009) most teachers will do this. The argument runs that females can get less class attention than males, less access to equipment such as computers and that tutors are often unaware of this. Petty (2009) also points out that learners from ethnic minorities and learners with learning difficulties and/or disabilities, shy learners or less able or disruptive learners may get unequal teaching in the classroom from some teachers. Moreover, the teachers are often unaware that this is happening.

Teaching is a 'craft' like any profession. In order to be as 'inclusive' as possible it is important to be aware of the possible 'pitfalls' in order to provide yourself with the best opportunity of avoiding them. As a teacher you will need to be aware of some strategies that can help you to address potential inequality at a practical level. According to Gravells and Simpson (2009) there are a number of ways that you can do this throughout your teaching. Examples include taking the time to learn the names of your children and use these names regularly to make each child feel fully included in the learning process. It is also important to negotiate and set 'ground rules' for behaviour within the classroom, beginning with the use of appropriate icebreakers to help to set the expected parameters for acceptable and unacceptable behaviour. This ought to facilitate a mutually respective learning environment. During the delivery of the teaching sessions, time should be taken to discuss issues such as equality and diversity policies and equality issues in ways that the children understand. If possible you should plan for additional tutorial support for those children who need this. This objective can be achieved by reflecting on the children's background. You might want to introduce formative activities that get the children to write about their extended family and friends. This is a useful way of identifying the kind of background the children are coming from. Once you are in possession of this information you may be more capable of meeting the particular needs of the children. It is also important to ask the children about their experiences at identified points in the teaching year such as at the beginning, middle and end of each term to gauge their needs. As a trainee teacher you also need to be aware that some children may actually stereotype you and you should think carefully about the image you wish to project to your children during the learning process.

## Case study

David is 35 years old and is in his post-qualifying year a teacher. He may be considered to be unusual due to him being an 'early years' specialist, an area of teaching in which there are a minority of males. David is meeting his class of children who are aged 7–8 years of age. A number of the children in this class have behavioural difficulties. David decides that he will wear more 'formal dress' (a suit and a tie) to set the tone for the session and to create a 'professional impression'. As his relationship develops with the students over the coming weeks he may relax this dress code and begin to wear more casual clothing. Why do you think David is thinking like this?

### Practical reflection

Think about the way you dress for teaching? Does your appearance and personality change depending upon the subject you are teaching and the group of children you are working with? Select two different classes and explain why you choose to make this impression.

# Appraising the curriculum

The curriculum may be defined as a programme of learning undertaken by individuals and groups of learners. Who accesses the curriculum and why depends upon a range of complex issues. Some of these issues can include political agendas such as widening participation which has impacted heavily upon the early years curriculum in the United Kingdom in recent years with the integration of children with special educational needs into the curriculum. Other factors may be regarded as being more localized, such as personal factors, social factors and economic factors all or some of which may prevent children from accessing the curriculum. In order to promote inclusive learning it is important to be aware of potential barriers and have strategies in place to help potential learners to overcome them.

It may seem like a relatively routine process to plan a curriculum. A scheme of work is developed based upon the requirements of the curriculum. The reality may be different. The availability of resources, such as time, staffing and rooming/equipment can all impact upon the curriculum. The reality can mean that designing an inclusive curriculum can be a complex process as the needs of individual children have to be considered.

Inclusive practice is about differentiated practice, about providing the best possible opportunity for learning to take place for all children and matching what you teach to the individual learning needs of each child in the group. This can be a very complex process, and even with the best of intentions it is not always possible to do this. This is because there may be financial constraints on you as a teacher in respect of the resources you can access. It may not be possible to secure the most appropriate teaching room to deliver your curriculum. You may need to adapt your teaching strategies to fit in with the resources that are made available to you. You may not always have time to prepare your resources exactly as you wish and this means that you may need to be flexible in your style of teaching delivery. This may not be ideal, but a good teacher develops the ability to think on his or her feet and to adapt teaching and learning practice to make learning for all as accessible as possible.

There are lots of ways that you can gain information about how successful a curriculum delivery has been in order to enhance learning. As we have already seen, one important form of feedback comes from your children. How the children respond in school tells us how the curriculum has been received!

This feedback and quantitative data about school performance can provide a real and valuable basis for planning future curriculum change. We have also suggested that in order to review the curriculum it is useful to adopt some frameworks for reflection, such as Brookfield's (1985) critical lenses. This may enable you to review the curriculum by considering the learning experiences of yourself, your children and your fellow teachers. Considering these experiences can help you to redesign the curriculum so that it can become more inclusive for the future.

It is also important to become aware of key legislation such as the DDA (2005) in order to assess how your organizational practices provide equal opportunities in order to enhance learning. Children may not have an 'identified' learning difficulty or disability and this can cause a real dilemma for teachers. How can you plan a 'reasonable adjustment' when you are not sure what the requirements are? The initial response to this question may be to plan your delivery to be as inclusive as possible. You will always be required to respond to the needs of your learners and at times it is wise to take advice from more experienced practitioners if you are concerned about the progress of your learners. When thinking about other aspects of inclusion, stereotyping may be difficult to avoid on both the part of teachers and learners. You should try to avoid making 'snap' judgements, as far as you can, on your first impressions of any child. This means that you need to give yourself time to get to know your children in order to gain a better personal knowledge of them and their individual needs. It is important to become aware of the aspirations of your children as well as their cultural and religious beliefs. This can help you to form a more balanced judgement of the needs of your children and it should help you to plan for a truly inclusive curriculum for each child. You also need to remember that the initial image of yourself that you project to your children is likely to leave them with a lasting impression, so you need to consider carefully the image you wish to project to your learners.

## Summary of key points

Due to the nature of the teaching profession, there will always be pressures that influence the curriculum. It is important that we work as positively as possible within these constraints to promote as inclusive a learning experience as possible by using all the available resources at our disposal. Inclusive practice is about meeting the diverse needs of all of the children as far as possible. It is about using differentiated approaches in teaching and learning. Using a range of sources of information for reviewing and evaluating the curriculum is important so that you can then reflect fully on your curriculum delivery and plan for any future changes. There are legal frameworks that you have to work within as a teacher and you need to be aware of these, especially in relation to anticipating the specific needs of the children you teach. Becoming aware of all of these issues should in turn help you to enhance the learning for the good of your children.

## Self-assessment questions

### Question 1
How would you define inclusive practice?

### Question 2
What are some of the key planning considerations you need to make in the design of a truly inclusive curriculum? List them.

### Question 3
Reflecting on experiences of curriculum delivery are an important part of planning to improve future practice. Brookfield's critical lenses are one method of doing this. What are the four aspects of this process?

## Moving on feature

This chapter has introduced you to curriculum development for inclusive practice. Try to think of how the material in this chapter can be applied to help you to design inclusive curricula within different educational contexts in order to meet the needs of a variety of learning groups.

## Further reading

Clements, P. and Jones, J. (2005), *The Diversity Training Handbook: A Practical Guide to Understanding and Changing Attitudes*. London: Kogan Page.

Kelly, A. V. (2004), *The Curriculum: Theory and Practice* (5th edn). London: Sage.

# Research Methods and Early Childhood Studies

## Learning outcomes

After reading this chapter you should be able to:

- identify what the term 'research' means within the early years context;
- analyse some of the ways that the research process can be used by early years practitioners;
- critically appraise some of the ways that the research process can be applied to early years.

The chapter develops your knowledge and understanding of selected research processes that inform the early years context. These processes are especially relevant to your professional practice. Through applying research to the early years context it is possible to ensure that professional practice is as innovative as possible. This is because researching professional roles enables you to deepen your understanding of what is meant by the term 'best practice' within the early years context. The chapter content explores key aspects of the research process. A number of key research models are identified alongside the associated research methods that can be applied within the research process. The chapter also considers those aspects of good practice that are especially important if effective research is to happen. The research process is outlined, analysed and critically appraised in order to investigate how research methods can be applied to early years. As with previous chapters, there are formative activities that reinforce learning in relation to the main aspects of the research process.

# Defining research

## Reflective Task 6.1

What is your understanding of the word research?

### Feedback

Research is an important part of every academic discipline. The term means discovering new information about a subject. When we discover this new information it enables us to confirm or dispute whether previous understandings of academic matters still apply. We can say that there are two especially influential theories that have influenced research. These are the 'positivist' and 'interpretative' models of research. The two theoretical perspectives provide opposing models of research. The positivist perspective is scientific in its approach. This is because it recommends that the best way to gather research data is to adopt a scientific perspective in order to gather statistics and quantifiable data. In contrast, the interpretative perspective is non-scientific in its approach. Interpretative research attempts to gather the views and opinions of individuals in a non-statistical way. These narrative accounts are used to present individual interpretations of the social world. Both approaches to research are summarized in the following dictionary definition of research:

> Diligent and systematic inquiry or investigation into a subject in order to revise facts, theories, applications.
>
> (Online Dictionary)

Research is important for early years practitioners because it provides the opportunity to revise and reinforce understandings of the early years context. This means that being aware of the research process enables you to increase your knowledge of the latest findings about the factors influencing children and families.

# The research process

The research process is characterized by competing models of research. The previous section of the chapter refers to the positivist and interpretative models of research. Both of these paradigms have a distinctive philosophy of the research process. This means that the data-gathering methods that are chosen are influenced by the underlying research philosophy. Whereas the positivist approach to research emphasizes the importance of 'scientific processes' the interpretative perspective is non-scientific in its outlook. This results in data-gathering methods that are concerned with gathering non-scientific or qualitative data.

# Competing perspectives

In addition to the positivist and interpretative research perspectives, 'action research' is another influential research perspective. This research model emphasizes the importance of researching professional practice so that the findings can be used to influence future work. This approach to research is often used within education so that the findings can be applied to improve professional practice. These research perspectives are described as being in competition because they have a conflicting understanding of the research process and how this process should be applied.

# Research methods

Research methods refer to the data collection processes that are applied by researchers. The data that is gathered is in general either 'quantitative' (or statistical) or 'qualitative' (or non-statistical). The research methods employed by the researcher are either 'primary' (or the immediate work of the researcher) or 'secondary' (in other words using the findings of other published researchers). The techniques used to gather this data can include questionnaires, interviews, observations, focus groups, case studies and book-based research in 'learning resource centres'.

# Validity

Validity is a term that is often associated with quantitative research. When we refer to the validity of qualitative research we consider the acceptability of the research process. There are accepted conventions followed by academic researchers, for example being aware of ethical issues. This means that it is important for researchers to be able to identify what is accepted as being 'good practice' within research. Research should not be used to harm others. There should always be consent and openness within any research project. If these principles are not apparent this can mean that the research is not valid or acceptable.

Four types of validity are typically associated with quantitative research. These types of validity are 'face validity', 'content validity', 'empirical validity' and 'predictive validity'.

## Face validity

This aspect of validity asks whether the research methods within a research project are appropriate. For example, is the data that is gathered by an initial questionnaire used to generate further data or are the two processes unrelated? If the research methods are unrelated to each other the validity, or acceptability of the research can be questioned.

## Content validity

Content validity relates to the theoretical content of the research process. Have key concepts been covered by the research? If they have, this means that the research is more likely to be valid. Research projects consider previously published literature. This is one way of attempting to show that key concepts have been covered.

## Empirical validity

This aspect of validity considers whether the research data supports the research question in a positive way. Does the data that has been gathered answer the research question in enough depth and detail? Has sufficient data been gathered or is there a need for more data gathering if the research question is to be answered comprehensively?

## Predictive validity

This aspect of validity looks at whether or not accurate predictions for the future can be made as a result of the research. Have definite findings been obtained that give enough depth and substance to predict future developments for the research area?

# Reliability

'Reliability' is another research term that is typically associated with quantitative research processes. In qualitative research, reliability refers to the accuracy or otherwise of the research findings. The ideal is for the research to produce consistent findings. If the research is characterized by this consistency of findings over time this adds to the quality of the research process. Like validity, there are a number of different types of reliability that are traditionally associated with quantitative research.

## Inter-observer reliability

This example of reliability refers to different researchers finding similar research findings. The discovery of this 'pattern' means that the research process has identified consistent findings.

### Test–retest reliability

This form of reliability uses the same methodology to produce consistent findings on a number of occasions. Once more, it is the discovery of a 'pattern' within the research that means we can say that the research is reliable.

### Inter-item reliability

This type of reliability means that different research methods are used in order to produce consistent findings. As an example, questionnaire data may be used to inform a survey or experiment. If the findings from these research methods are consistent, this will add to the reliability of the research findings.

# Triangulation

This term has been popularized by Norman Denzin and Lincoln (2000). Triangulation means that the researcher uses at least two different ways of gathering research data. As an example, a researcher might use interviews and library research as the sources of data. As long as the data has been gathered effectively and there is depth and detail of content, the subsequent theory is more likely to be valid and reliable. Like 'reliability' and 'validity', there are different ways of showing that you have triangulation of data.

### Methodological triangulation

This type of triangulation is characterized by the researcher using many different but complementary research methods.

### Data triangulation

This form of triangulation draws on many different but complementary sets of data.

### Investigator triangulation

This form of triangulation uses the research findings of many different researchers.

## Theory triangulation

This type of triangulation uses a number of different but relevant theories to interpret the research findings.

# Research ethics

Researchers need to be aware of ethical good practice. Ethics refers to applying moral principles in order to ensure that the research subjects are never harmed by the research process. Opie (2004, p. 25) defines research ethics as 'the application of moral principles to prevent harming or wronging others, to promote the good, to be respectful and fair'. Ethics needs to be considered at all points of the study, from the design of the research question to interpreting the results, and presenting the findings.

## Designing the research question

It is important to ask yourself what you want to know and why you want to research into your chosen topic. This is so that you can confirm that you have a justifiable interest in your area of research. If your research is in any way 'experimental' it is important to consider the implications for those involved. Opie (2004, pp. 25–6) emphasizes the importance of asking yourself about the 'potential consequences' of the research.

## Procedures for data collection

When you are gathering research data, it is important to ensure that you never ask your research participants anything that you would not want to be asked. It is also important to make sure that you never ask people to do anything that you would not want to be asked to do. Opie (2004, p. 27) considers that these two points are 'the acid test' of good practice within research.

## Research relationships

It is important to remember that you have a moral responsibility to the people that you are working with. Make sure that you do not manipulate the research relationship to get 'good data'. It is also important to be aware of the power relationship that exists between you and the research subjects. Opie

(2004, p. 29) draws attention to the powerful position that you can be in as a researcher and the powerless position that may be experienced by those being 'researched'.

## Data interpretation and analysis

It is important to be aware of any theoretical frameworks or value systems that might influence your data interpretation and analysis. The research process can be complicated and it is important to acknowledge challenges in answering research questions as opposed to making the process appear 'neat' and 'uncomplicated'. Opie (2004, pp. 30–1) emphasizes that protecting research subjects in written accounts is especially important if ethical principles are to be maintained.

## Data dissemination

When you present your research findings it is important to ensure that your research participants' anonymity is protected. The most essential principle is for you to avoid harming anyone during the research process. Opie (2004, p. 32) recommends that researchers always have to consider whether 'the ends justify the means' during the research process.

Table 6.1 summarizes the essential points of good practice that need to be remembered if good practice within research is to be maintained.

From this initial discussion about the research process we can now explore the concept 'methodology'.

**Table 6.1** 'Remember' research ethics

| |
| --- |
| **R**emain true to your data in order to maintain professional integrity. |
| **E**nsure that the physical, social, psychological well-being of research participants is never adversely affected. |
| **M**ake your research participants know how far they will be given anonymity and confidentiality. |
| **E**xcessive covert or 'hidden' research violates the principles of informed consent. |
| **M**ake no threats to confidentiality and anonymity of research data. |
| **B**e especially careful if your research subjects are vulnerable because of age, disability, physical and/or mental health. |
| **E**xtra care is required if your research involves children. The consent of parent and child must be sought. |
| **R**esearch participants need to know that they have the right to refuse to participate. |

## Reflective Task 6.2

What do you think the word 'methodology' means?

### Feedback

The word 'methodology' sounds like the word 'method'. A way of explaining this word is to think about studying different ways of doing research. There are different research methods or ways of completing research. We have previously identified the difference between the 'positivist' and 'interpretative' approaches to doing research. Whereas the positivist approach places an emphasis on 'scientific' methods, the interpretative approach is 'non-scientific' in its emphasis. 'Methodology' is a word that means the study of methods of data collection. It is important to emphasize that in addition to differing theoretical approaches to gathering data, there are a number of different research methods. These research methods gather quantitative (numerical) and/or qualitative (non-numerical) data. The sort of data that is gathered depends on the approach of the researcher. If you have a scientific approach to your research question you are likely to gather quantitative data. If you are non-scientific in your research approach you are likely to gather qualitative data. The methods that are used can include questionnaires, surveys, interviews, observation, focus groups, experiments and library research. These research methods can be used in isolation or combined together to produce comprehensive research findings. The number of methods being used depends upon the nature of the research question and the specific research objectives.

We can now add more detail to our discussion of research perspectives and data collection methods. This a way of setting the scene before we look at how the research process can be applied to early years practice.

# The research models

Table 6.2 gives a summary of three influential models of research with a brief description of their key features.

**Table 6.2** Research models

| Research model | Key features |
| --- | --- |
| Positivist | This perspective was popularized initially by David Hume in the eighteenth century. It emphasizes the importance of 'scientific' approaches to understanding the world. |
| Interpretative | This school of thought has been popularized by Edmund Husserl. It emphasizes the importance of non-scientific approaches to the research process. |
| Action research | This model of research has been popularized by Kurt Lewin since the 1940s. It emphasizes the importance of researching professional practice. The objective of the research is to improve future professional practice. |

These models of research are especially useful to early years because of the influence they have had in shaping the research process. If you are working in early years you will need to influence practitioners by drawing attention to examples of good professional practice. Knowledge and awareness of research about early years will help you to develop as a professional. As with the psychological and sociological perspectives we have looked at thus far, the origins of the ideas in these models of research go back to some of the important philosophical ideas that have influenced Western thought. Bryman (2004, p. 11) considers that the emphasis that is placed upon scientific practice within the positivist perspective goes back to the ideas of the Enlightenment. This idea is central to the positivist model of research so it can be claimed that the perspective has its intellectual origins in this classical thought. The interpretivist research paradigm emphasizes the importance of individuals establishing creative meaning with the social world. Bryman (2004, p. 13) equates this approach to research with 'phenomenology'. This in turn links the perspective to the ideas within humanism and interactionism. In other words the genesis of the perspective's dominant idea can be linked to these theoretical perspectives. A summary of each of the three research perspectives follows. A definition of each of the key perspectives is given, key figures influencing the perspective are identified and central terms within each perspective are explained.

## Positivist research

The positivist model of research is based on scientific principles. David Hume is associated with this perspective. This research model tends to be grounded in measurable or 'statistical' data. This means that the perspective is based on precise measurements that test theoretical perspectives by applying reason to identify whether or not the theory can be proven or not. Research that is based on this perspective usually begins with a hypothesis proposing a correlation or relationship. The objective of the subsequent research process is to identify whether or not the hypothesis is correct. This then enables the researcher to produce broad generalizations that allow scientific theory to be generated.

### Applying positivist research to early years

Positivist research is often used to reveal what is happening in the lives of children and families in the United Kingdom. There are numerous examples of where statistics are used to either prove or disprove an argument. Examples include the House of Commons Work and Pensions findings of 2003–4 revealing that 8 per cent of UK children do not have a warm waterproof coat. These findings are quantified in a 'scientific' way in order to answer a hypothesis. A frequent strategy within this positivist approach is to present statistical findings in combinations so that a set of statistics appear to be reinforcing an answer to a hypothesis. In the above example, other statistics are used to support the argument that poverty is a significant issue affecting many UK children and families. The report goes on to cite that '20% of UK children live in poverty for over three years'. These statistics are used to present a definite answer to an aspect of research. They are statistics that are used to present a large-scale general answer to question.

## Interpretative research

Interpretivist research places an emphasis upon the importance of interpreting human experience. The perspective has been popularized by Edmund Husserl. In many respects the perspective is opposed to the positivist model of research. Instead of emphasizing the importance of 'scientific analysis', 'hypotheses' and 'surveys', interpretative research focuses on individuals and how they experience the social world. This means that data gathering is regarded as reflecting the researcher's personal engagement with the research process. The process becomes as important as the data that has been gathered as there is the acknowledgement of the creativity of both the researcher and the research subjects. The consequence of this approach is that research becomes more narrative and less statistical.

### Applying interpretative research to early years

In his book *Local Knowledge* (1993), Clifford Geertz argues that 'largeness of mind' comes from reflecting on how we interact with others. This process of reflecting on interaction is at the centre of the interpretivist approach to methodology. It can be argued that some of the most profound accounts of early years have come from the interpretative model of doing research. This is revealed in Green and Hogan's (2005) book *Researching Children's Experience: Approaches and Methods*. The book is grounded in important themes such as 'anthropological and sociological perspectives', 'ethnographic research methods' and 'phenomenological approaches to research with children'. The authors do acknowledge that the positivist approach to research is also important. As Green and Hogan (2005, p. 5) say, 'if we want to know how many children have experienced the death of a parent we must collect appropriate statistics'. It is, however, implied that a statistical focus may not account for the rich variety of experience within the early years context. It can be suggested that this is a particularly important benefit of the interpretative approach to research. The creativity of children and early years practitioners may be captured by placing an emphasis on researching the process of interaction.

## Action research

This research perspective has been popularized by Kurt Lewin. The central purpose of action research is to improve professional practice through researching into aspects of 'best practice'. Action research is developmental because the central aim of the research is to investigate practice with a view to developing professional roles. This means that action research does not attempt to discover general findings. It is research that is characterized by findings that are 'particular' and 'specific'. Action research is one of the most important forms of professional research. It is a research process that has been described as being 'cyclical' and not linear. This is because the research process involves data gathering, reviewing the data that has been collected, planning for new action and in turn implementing new action.

### Applying action research to early years

Action research can be applied to early years by reflecting on professional practice. If there are elements of practice that are not working it is possible to research what needs to be done to make improvements to this situation. It is also possible to identify the aspects of professional practice that are working well in order to inform future professional work. As the early years context is an area of education that can be characterized by innovative government policy initiatives it appears to be constantly adapting to the latest interpretation of 'best practice'. This means that it is important to have action researchers who can inform and influence future policy initiatives.

---

### Reflective Task 6.3

Which of these research approaches do you think is the best approach to adopt as a researcher?

> **Feedback**
>
> The answer to this question is that the approach that is adopted depends upon the nature of your research question. If you are doing research on the number of children under 7 years of age who have experienced family breakdown, it may be more appropriate to adopt a positivist approach in order to gather statistics so that a 'large-scale' analysis can be completed. This is not to say that this research question could not be answered by a smaller-scale focus that looks at the experiences of a few research participants. The approach that is adopted depends upon what the researcher wants to answer and how they want to respond to the research question. It may be that a combination of methods is used so that in addition to gathering statistics there are also reflective accounts that are interpretative. In other words the different research models are not necessarily opposed to one another. They can be used together to produce a comprehensive answer to the research question.

# The research methods

Research methods gather data that is either qualitative (non-statistical) or quantitative (statistical) or a combination of both. If you are doing research, a range of methods are available to you. The methods that you will use for your research depend upon the nature of the research question you want to answer. If you have a small-scale area of focus you are likely to use fewer data collection methods. This may mean that you are inclined to use interpretative methods for gathering your data because you do not want to provide broad generalizations from your research. In other words the research perspective that is adopted and the methods that are used are entirely driven by the research question and its associated objectives.

In general, the positivist approach is considered to be a structured scientific approach. This means that a deductive approach is adopted that tests a specific hypothesis. The research process is concerned with exploring the relationships that exist between particular variables. If one adopts this research perspective it is likely that the methods that are chosen are those that can gather large amounts of statistical data that can be quantified and used as a basis for broad conclusions.

In contrast, the research methods that are used within the interpretative perspective are relatively unstructured. The research is more likely to be 'inductive' or open-ended in nature. The research methods are concerned with identifying the meaning of social interaction. These 'negotiated meanings' are used to establish theories that attempt to explain social interaction.

## Example research methods

A number of research methods are available to researchers. The previous section has identified that the type of methods that are used for data gathering depend on the nature of the research question. Some of the popular data-gathering techniques are discussed in this section.

### Experiments

This type of data collection method is used within the positivist model of research. Experiments adopt a 'cause and effect' approach by seeking to prove or disprove a hypothesis.

### Surveys

Surveys are used in order to 'pool' or obtain information about attitudes, beliefs and behaviours. Surveys are usually large scale and they tend to be associated with the positivist perspective and its attempt to answer a research question in a 'scientific' manner.

### Focus groups

Kreuger (1994) defines focus groups as being small structured groups (between 4 and 12 people) that are facilitated by the researcher. The aim of the focus group is to generate detailed discussion about an issue of relevance to the research question. This data is gathered via a semi-structured question and answer discussion. Kreuger (1994) emphasizes the importance of providing a permissive and non-threatening environment in order to generate detailed data.

### Interviews

Gillham (2000) defines an interview as a conversation between two people in which the interviewer seeks particular responses from the interviewee. There are different types of interview. There are structured interviews that are rigidly structured, with a set of questions that all the interviewees are expected to answer. There are semi-structured interviews where a series of prompts are used with the interviewees in order to facilitate more flexible discussion about particular issues. There are also unstructured interviews where the discussion is about an area of focus with no prior prompts provided by the interviewer.

## *Observation*

In addition to the different sorts of interviews, there are also different forms of observation. We can distinguish between 'participant' and 'structured' observation. Structured observation is defined as being a quantitative analysis of actions whereas participant observation is regarded as being a qualitative engagement in interaction. In other words the type of observation that is done will link to the research paradigm that is being adopted by the researcher.

---

### Reflective Task 6.4

What are the advantages and disadvantages of questionnaires and interviews?

#### Feedback

All of the above research methods have advantages and disadvantages. The methods that are used depend upon the research question that has been selected and the research objectives.

Questionnaires have the advantage of being able to gather quantitative and qualitative data. This is possible if you have a combination of closed and open questions. The 'yes/no' closed questions can be used to produce statistical data. The 'open' questions that request the views and opinions of research subjects can be used to gather qualitative data. Another advantage of questionnaires is that they can be issued to a large number of research subjects. If the questionnaire is well designed this can mean that a large amount of data is gathered relatively quickly. Many students doing research find that a questionnaire is a useful way of beginning a research study. There is the possibility of gathering much initial data about the chosen area of study.

A disadvantage of questionnaires is that the questions can be misinterpreted by the research subjects. This means that it is important to ensure that the questions are written in a clear and unambiguous way. It is also important to ensure that the questions are organized in a logical way so that the research subjects can understand the rationale behind the questionnaire's design.

Interviews have the advantage of providing potentially 'rich' and detailed information about the research topic. If a researcher is interviewing a research subject for half an hour there is the possibility of gathering much data. It is also possible to treat the interviewee as an 'individual' so their views and opinions are respected during the research process.

A disadvantage of interviews is that they are potentially time-consuming. This means that you are unlikely to gather a large number of respondent views in a typical interview schedule. This in turn results in the research becoming small scale and localized. It may then be impossible to establish a general theory that can be applied on a broad scale. Another potential disadvantage of the interview process is the influence of the interviewer on the interviewee. The interviewee may give answers to 'please' the interviewer as opposed to really saying what they think about particular issues.

# Analysing data

We have previously identified that there are quantitative (or statistical) and qualitative (non-statistical) sets of data. Once the data has been gathered it needs to be analysed. This section of the chapter outlines some of the important aspects of the data analysing process.

Two example strands of data processing include 'quantitative data analysis' and 'qualitative data analysis'. Within quantitative data analysis we can distinguish between 'descriptive' and 'inferential' statistics. Whereas descriptive statistics identify the nature of the data findings, inferential statistics are used to generate theory from statistical data. Within qualitative data analysis we can use what is referred to as 'theme analysis' to generate theory from the qualitative data.

## Descriptive statistics

Descriptive statistics are used to describe the numerical data that has been gathered. It makes sense that the first step in any statistical analysis is to describe the data that has been obtained. There are different types of descriptive statistics and these include frequency distributions, measures of central tendency and measures of dispersion.

### *Frequency distributions*

These descriptive statistics are used to describe the frequency of particular categories within a data set. This is exemplified in Table 6.3.

**Table 6.3** Frequency distributions

| Social class | Frequency | Percentage |
|---|---|---|
| 1 | 7 | 17.5 |
| 2 | 15 | 37.5 |
| 3 | 8 | 20 |
| 4 | 6 | 15 |
| 5 | 4 | 10 |
| **Total** | **40** | **100** |

## Measures of central tendency

These descriptive statistics provide a single figure to represent a data set as effectively as possible. Three popular ways of doing this are by presenting a 'mode', a 'median' and a 'mean'. The mode represents the most frequently occurring statistic, the median is the middle score in the data set and the mean is the arithmetic average score within a data set.

## Measures of dispersion

Numerical data sets have differing degrees of internal variability. This means that each set of numerical data can differ according to the range that has been obtained. The 'range' in this instance refers to the highest and lowest scores within a set of data. An important term within this category of statistical analysis is 'standard deviation'. This term can be used to indicate how close or otherwise the statistical findings are to the average value. If you report that '68 per cent of all measurements fall within 1 standard deviation of the average' this indicates how close the data set is to the average value that has been obtained. In other words if the average was '9' this would mean that 68 per cent of the findings are between 7 and 10.

# Levels of measurement

Within statistical data sets there are four different levels of measurement that are used to interpret the information that has been gathered. These levels of measurement are referred to as 'nominal, ordinal, interval and ratio' measurements.

## Nominal measurement

This term refers to measurements that are arranged according to categories. An example of nominal measurement can be seen with the following example of social class and its division into upper class, upper middle class, middle class, lower middle class, upper working class and lower working class.

## Ordinal measurement

Ordinal measurement allows the data to be arranged in a numbered series. An example of ordinal measurement occurs if the respondents' attitudes are measured, with '1' representing 'most popular', '2' representing 'neutral' and '3' representing 'least popular'.

### Interval measurement

This form of measurement has equal intervals between the points on the measurement scale. If you use whole numbers to present your statistical data you are using interval measurement as the basis of your theoretical conclusions. An example of this type of measurement is temperature where the range might be from –20 to 30°C. If you were researching how climate differences influence types of play on a global scale you might use interval measurement to present your findings.

### Ratio measurement

This type of measurement is similar to interval measurement but it takes into consideration the intervals on the measurement scale in relation to 'absolute zero'. An example of ratio measurement can be seen with test scores where they are understood in relation to a score between 0 and 100.

### Level of measurement and graphs

The type of measurement that is chosen in turn influences how the data should be presented. This is outlined in Table 6.4.

## Pie charts, bar charts and scattergrams

Using charts to present your findings can be an effective way of presenting the data that you have obtained. The subsequent section gives three examples of a pie chart (Figure 6.1), a bar chart (Figure 6.2) and a scattergram (Figure 6.3).

## Inferential statistics

These statistics differ from descriptive statistics because they are used to generate theory as opposed to report findings. Inferential statistics look for the differences and the relationships between sets of data. These differences

**Table 6.4** Type of measurement and choice of graph

| Type of measurement | Pie chart | Bar chart | Scattergram |
|---|---|---|---|
| Nominal | * | * | |
| Ordinal | * | * | * |
| Interval | | | * |
| Ratio | | | * |

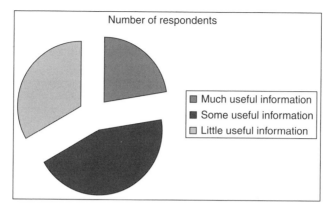

**Figure 6.1** Example pie chart.

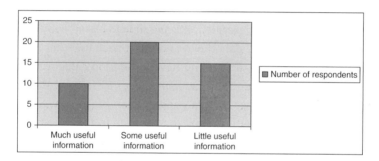

**Figure 6.2** Example bar chart.

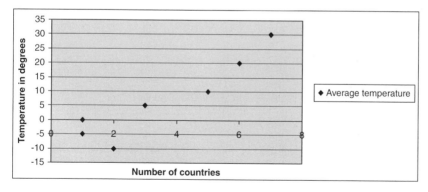

**Figure 6.3** Example scattergram.

and relationships are then used to generate interpretations of the data. Alan Bryman and D. Cramer (1997, pp. 4–5) define inferential statistics as enabling the researcher to demonstrate that the results from a sample of the data set are likely to be found in any other random sample of the data.

## Qualitative data analysis

The first stage in analysing qualitative data is to describe the data. You might want to present the main research findings and then write a paragraph about each of these main findings. By doing this you will be developing what Geertz (1973) refers to as 'thick description'. This means that you are developing thorough and comprehensive descriptions of the phenomena that are being studied. This 'thick description' gets its label from the depth of detail that is included about context, intentions, meanings and process.

Once the data has been described, it is possible to classify your findings, or in other words break the data down and put it back together in a meaningful way. This might mean that you have to develop categories in order to organize and classify your data. Categorizing or classifying data enables you to 'funnel' your findings so that concepts can be compared and contrasted. This then enables you to look for patterns in the data that can be used to inform your theory. It provides you with the opportunity to explore the links that exist between categories. This in turn allows you to develop explanations that can explain these associations. Once you have analysed your qualitative data in this way you can then develop theory from your data.

### Reflective Task 6.5

Think about each of the stages of the research process and suggest how you might investigate attitudes to 'healthy eating' within a local primary school.

### Feedback

One of the most important parts of the research process is to choose a manageable research focus. You can do this through thinking carefully about the title of your research. In the above example, it is important to show that you are not going to embark on a research project that is too big and unmanageable. If you have a title like 'Critical Appraisal of Attitudes Towards Healthy Eating in a Local Primary School' you have a manageable focus for your research because you are doing your research on one organization. It is also important to ensure that your research objectives are manageable and that they show that you are aware of the importance of 'identifying, analysing and critically assessing' relevant issues. Never have too many objectives as it is hard to show that all the objectives have been achieved. In the above example research question you might have the following three research objectives:

- identify attitudes to healthy eating in a local primary school;
- analyse attitudes to healthy eating in a local primary school;
- critically assess recent policy developments in view of the research findings.

Before beginning the research, you need to think about the research paradigm that will be applied to your study. In the above example question, all three of the research models that we have referred to in the chapter are relevant to the question. This is because it is possible to gather statistics about healthy eating so the positivist model of research is relevant. In identifying 'attitudes', the interpretative paradigm is being applied. If the research findings are being used to make recommendations about how practice can be improved in the future, we can also say that the research question links to 'action research'.

Once you have identified your research paradigm, you need to think about how you will gather your data. The above research question can be answered through applying a combination of quantitative and qualitative data. You could design a questionnaire that has both closed and open questions in order to gather statistical and non-statistical data. The closed questions, with their 'yes/no' responses can be quantified. If you have a question like 'have you worked in the school for less than 5 years?' you can give a descriptive statistic that summarizes this finding within your research report. If you include an open question such as 'what are your views on healthy eating?' you can in turn provide the attitudes and views of your respondents. In order to show that you are aware of the importance of triangulation you could develop this initial questionnaire into a series of semi-structured interviews with five of the respondents who completed the questionnaire. You could also do secondary research on the internet to find out about other published accounts that link to your own research. This will help the validity and reliability of your findings. If you also show that all your research participants have had their confidentiality respected you can also say that you are aware of the importance of ethical principles.

## Practical task

When you are in an early years setting take a research diary and make a note of which aspects of practice could be studied as an example of action research. Think about what you would need to do so that the research was valid and reliable.

We can now complete the chapter by focusing our discussion on critically appraising the research process by thinking about its value for early years.

# Critical appraisal of the research process

The sort of research model that you use and the methods that are applied to your research are, as we have emphasized, determined by the nature of your research question and your research objectives. It is also important to consider the advantages and disadvantages of the different research models and methods.

## Appraising positivist research

The positivist model of research has the advantage of being a large-scale approach to answering the research question. The surveys and experiments that are conducted within this research framework will typically generate much data that can be arranged to present a seemingly thorough answer to the research question. Another advantage of this approach to research is the emphasis that is placed on being 'objective' and 'scientific'. Bryman (2004, p. 11) argues that within this perspective, the research must always be conducted in a way that is 'value free'. A further advantage of the scientific nature of the positivist approach is the 'definite' nature of the findings. Through applying statistics, you are able to give a definite answer to your research question. In appraising the value of the positivist approach to research Bryman (2004, p. 13) argues that a difficulty with this research model rests with the confusion over the difference between the positivist perspective and scientific research. In other words, is this model of research the same as 'scientific philosophy' or different? If the research model is different, how does it differ? Bryman also suggests that it is also not clear whether it is appropriate to study 'society' in a scientific way. This is because human beings interact in ways that are often contrary to the scientific model of the world.

## Appraising interpretative research

The interpretative model of research places an emphasis on the 'phenomenology' of human experience. Bryman (2004, p. 13) summarizes this idea as *a philosophy that is concerned with the question of how individuals make sense of the world around them and how in particular the philosopher should bracket out preconceptions in his or her grasp of the world.* An advantage of this model of research is the attention that is given to the creativity of the research process. This means that interpretivism argues that researching human beings is an entirely different process to 'scientific research'. As opposed to looking for large-scale general theories, the researcher is looking at small-scale interpretations of social meaning. The advantage of this approach is that it is possible to recognize the profound nature of human interaction. This suggests that a scientific approach, with its emphasis on 'reason' and 'rationality', may miss the creative and inventive nature of human interaction. A difficulty of this model of research is seen in the Geertz (1988, p. 2) quote that the research process can become akin to 'the lady sawed in half' that is 'done but never really done at all'. As a result of the emphasis that is placed upon 'interpretation' the intensity of the research process can mean that the research findings are so localized and small scale that it is impossible to generate any general theory. This point is reinforced by Bryman (2004, p. 16) who argues that interpretivist research represents 'tendencies rather than definite points of correspondence'. If this argument is developed you can challenge any interpretative research by claiming that the findings are representative of 'views and opinions' but little else. This can mean that it becomes difficult to generate theory from the research findings because of their small-scale, intense and localized nature.

## Appraising action research

Action research can appear to be a diverse and broad approach to the research process. This is acknowledged by Bryman (2004, p. 277). This can mean that the researcher becomes a central part of the field of study. The advantage of this characteristic of action research, is that it enables the collection of 'rich' data about the chosen topic. Paolo Freire (1970) draws attention to the impact that action research has had on developing educational practice. The cyclical nature of the action research process also means that the research model is not 'linear'. It is opposed to the 'thesis, antithesis, synthesis' model of thought that appears to have influenced the positivist and interpretative research models. This means that there is the possibility of constantly comparing research findings as the emphasis is placed on gathering as much data as possible in order to inform future practice. Chambers (1983) draws attention to a difficulty with the action research process as a result of its inherently political nature. The researcher is intimately connected with the research process as a practitioner in the area of research. This can mean that it becomes difficult to gain an impartial view.

## Appraising quantitative research

We have said that 'methodology' refers to the model of research that you are using and the data collection methods that are being applied to answer the research question. Each data collection method has advantages and disadvantages. Bryman (2004, p. 62) defines quantitative research as 'entailing the collection of numerical data'. An advantage of having quantitative data is that it can be used to generate statistical findings that appear to offer definite answers to specific research questions. If you read a research report and it states that '80 per cent of UK children aged 7–8 enjoy school' this appears to be a clear and unambiguous finding. Bryman (2004, p. 78) does, however, criticize quantitative researchers because 'they fail to distinguish people and social institutions from the world of nature'. This is because the processes that are used in analysing the social world are no different to those that are being used to analyse the natural world. We have already said that human beings have the capacity for inventiveness and creativity. This can mean that a statistical analysis of human behaviour does not account for every aspect of human interaction. This leads Bryman (2004, p. 78) to propose that quantitative measurement 'possesses an artificial and spurious sense of precision and accuracy'. It can also lead to a somewhat static portrayal of human life as the analysis is structured by statistics. Although it would be wrong to say that quantitative research is 'wrong' these criticisms need to be taken into consideration if you are adopting a quantitative approach to your research question.

## Appraising qualitative research

Qualitative research is characterized by its focus on non-statistical data. Bryman (2004, p. 266) defines qualitative research as being 'concerned with words rather than with numbers'. We have said that an advantage of this approach is that it embraces the creativity of the research process. This means that the research process is understood in relation to 'negotiated meanings'. Qualitative research accounts can be detailed, enjoyable accounts that outline the interaction between the researcher and the research subjects. The criticism of this process is based on the difficulties that are associated with developing general theory from a small-scale qualitative analysis. Bryman (2004, p. 284) argues that qualitative research can be 'too subjective'. This can mean that it becomes difficult to replicate a qualitative study because the research process is so particular to the area of study. This in turn means that it is very hard to generalize and give coherent answers to large-scale research questions. The involvement of the researcher within the research process can also mean that it is difficult to see what the researcher actually did and how the conclusions of the research were reached.

# Example research project in Early Childhood Studies

Here is a recent research project in Early Childhood Studies that has been accepted for publication in the international journal *Professional Development in Education*. The summary of the research context and its associated methodology give an indication of how to write your research if you want to see your work published in academic journals.

## Research context

The research sample constituted 330 students and 26 academic tutors who are associated with the Early Years Sector Endorsed Foundation Degree (EYSEFD) at six UK Higher Education Institutions (HEIs). The research project has gathered the views and opinions of the students and tutors on student study skills needs and pedagogical practitioner Continuing Professional Development (CPD) needs since October 2009. The students completed a study skills questionnaire at the end of their level five (or second-year) programme study. Ninety-eight per cent of the students in the research sample are female and all of the students in the research sample work with children and families in a variety of statutory and private child care settings. Sixty per cent of the participants are employed in the statutory (or state) sector whereas 40 per cent are based in private settings. These child care settings include statutory schools, Sure Start centres, private nurseries and statutory health settings. Twenty out of the 26 staff working on the academic programme are female. Many of these staff have previously worked in health, education and social care contexts prior to teaching in HEIs. The gender balance of both students and staff confirms what Parker-Rees et al. (2004, p. 128) refers to as 'the overwhelmingly female' children's workforce in the United Kingdom and beyond. Table 6.5 outlines the specific employment settings of the pedagogical practitioners who constitute the research sample.

**Table 6.5** Employment settings of the pedagogical practitioners in the research sample

| Type of setting | Percentage of practitioners in the research sample employed in the setting |
| --- | --- |
| Private nurseries | 40 |
| Sure start settings | 29 |
| Statutory primary schools | 25 |
| National Health Service (NHS) settings | 6 |

The research has been completed on the EYSEFD qualification. This vocational degree attempts to develop the skills of the UK children's workforce by taking into consideration the recommendations of the CWDC (Children's Workforce Development Council). To obtain 'sector endorsement', the HEI needs to demonstrate to the CWDC that key UK governmental policies for working with children and families are incorporated into the academic programme content. These policies and initiatives are listed by the CWDC (2010) as being 'Every Child Matters'; the EYFS (Early Years Foundation Stage); the EYPS (Early Years Professional Standards); and the Common Core of Skills and Knowledge for the Children's Workforce. The confirmation of 'sector endorsement' is evidence that the HEIs are basing their academic programmes upon the standards that are inherent in the above policies and initiatives. In order to retain the title of 'sector endorsement', each HEI programme coordinator is obliged to send the CWDC a report (using a template devised by them) that outlines how the academic programme is reinforcing the recommendations of the previously cited policies and initiatives. This means that the EYSEFD is a programme that can be defined as being what Lucas (2007) has previously referred to as 'standards-driven'. This is because in order to receive endorsement from the CWDC, the academic programme needs to make reference to the above policies and initiatives (or standards). Meeting the criteria for 'sector endorsement' from the CWDC confirms the award of 'senior practitioner status' on those students who complete the EYSEFD.

The academic programme studied by the students in this research project has eight modules that are taught over 2 years. Six of the modules are delivered through a combination of lectures and seminars. The other two modules require the students to develop a 'Professional Development Portfolio' (or PDP) where they reflect on aspects of the academic programme in respect of their professional work. The programme's module content is based on sociological, psychological, pedagogical and social policy content. Each of the initial modules introduces content that is reinforced by the modules that are studied in the second year of the programme. The programme is assessed through a combination of essays, reports, case-study reflections and portfolio reflections. The assessments encourage the students to develop reflective practice.

The PDP modules studied in years one and two of the programme, represent a combination of academic tasks linked to the programme module content, alongside reflections on professional practice within the work place. Half of the academic programme is assessed by this module. A mentor in the work place is assigned to each student in order to encourage the students to reflect on their professional practice. The programme staff began to apply Janet Hale's (2008) recommendation of curriculum mapping from October 2009. This has led to 'study skills' activities being incorporated (or 'mapped') into each taught module. In the first year of the degree, students are taught how to write essays and reports alongside how to develop presentation skills and critical thinking skills. In the second year of the programme the students are taught to reflect on presentation skills and use IT (Information Technology) creatively within pedagogy. The current programme specification was approved in October 2009 so this is why the research project began at this time. The research project has explored the perceived impact of this pedagogical approach on the CPD needs of these pedagogical practitioners within the children's workforce. The research question is:

'How does the integration of taught study skills within the EYSEFD impact on CPD within Early Years?'

The specific research objectives that have been considered are:

1.  Identification of how the CPD needs of pedagogical practitioners in early years working for the children's workforce in England are influenced by integrating taught study skills into the EYSEFD.
2.  Analysis and appraisal of this curriculum initiative for the future development of effective CPD for practitioners working for the children's workforce in England and beyond.

## Methodological approach

The researchers mirrored previous research processes that appear to have been successful in identifying professional CPD needs within pedagogy. These studies include Brookes (2005), Ingleby and Hunt (2008), Ingleby (2010) and Simpson (2010). The findings from this questionnaire data were used to identify emerging research themes. The researchers adopted Geertz's (1973) 'thick description' methodological approach. This methodological strategy can be used to link primary and secondary data collection strategies together in order to provide a thorough answer to the research question. Audi (1995) argues that Geertz was influenced by the philosophy of Gilbert Ryle in developing this idea of thick description. Just as Ryle argues against the Cartesian separation of the 'mind' and the 'body', so Geertz argues against isolating data collection methods. The ideal of thick description is for primary and secondary data sets to support and develop emerging research themes.

In this research project the questionnaire design was informed by the methodological approach employed by Brookes (2005), Ingleby and Hunt (2008) and Ingleby (2010). The application of 'quota and dimensional sampling' that occurs in some of these previous studies was also mirrored within the research design. Bryman (2004) explains quota sampling as representing the attempt made to gather the views of all the research participants. The dimensional sampling was used for the focus group discussions. Bryman (2004) explains dimensional sampling as representing the attempt made by researchers to select key participants who can comment on the main emerging research themes. Two focus group discussions occurred in order to develop the main themes that emerged from the questionnaire data and enable a thick description of the research objectives. Whereas Brookes (2005) develops his questionnaire data with a series of one-to-one informal interviews with six participants, this research process applied a focus group approach in order to generate a discussion forum about meeting CPD needs. This is because the researchers agree with Kreuger (1994) and Munday (2006) who argue that focus groups can facilitate a permissive, non-threatening environment in order to generate rich discussions about CPD. In the focus groups the researchers selected those participants who in their opinion were most likely to give detailed comments on the issues being discussed within the focus group. The first focus group included the six HEI programme leaders and the six student representatives of the programme. The two main themes that previously emerged from the questionnaire data (the importance of developing IT skills and the consequences of standards-driven curricula) were used to structure this focus group discussion. The second focus group occurred with the programme leaders. This discussion was centred on how the programme's level 4 and 5 PDP modules could be developed to meet the CPD needs of early years pedagogical practitioners.

These PDP modules had been identified previously by the programme's student representatives and programme leaders as essential components of the academic programme as they represent a combination of academic tasks alongside reflection on professional practice. As a consequence of this synthesis of academic and professional practice it can be argued that these modules are especially important to meeting the practitioners' CPD needs. Developing the formal curriculum content is a responsibility of the programme leaders and not the programme's student representatives so this is why these individuals were chosen for the second focus group.

## Summary of key points

This chapter has given an outline of the research process by considering research in relation to early years. Doing research may not be 'easy' but it is not an impossible challenge. The secret of successful research appears to be being prepared. As opposed to doing 'hasty research' it is important to consider which model of research you are going to apply and which research methods you are going to use in order to gather your data. These approaches will be determined by your research question and its associated objectives. The rest of the research process resembles providing the evidence necessary to win an argument. You need to gather enough data to produce an answer that is reliable and valid. For the validity or authenticity of your data to be accepted you need to make sure that you are aware of the ethics of research. Always ensure that no harm results from your research. If these guidelines are followed doing research can be one of the most enjoyable aspects of early years. It is also one of the most important ways of understanding the early years context. This makes doing research especially relevant to Early Childhood Studies.

## Self-assessment questions

### Question 1
What are the names of three research models that are relevant to early years?

### Question 2
How can early years workers apply the research process to help children and maximize their professional practice?

*Question 3*
Give an example strength and weakness of each of the three research models outlined in this chapter.

## Moving on feature

This chapter has introduced you to the research process. Try to think of a research question and research objectives that would link to one of the main chapters in the book.

## Further reading

Bryman, A. (2004), *Social Research Methods*. Oxford: Oxford University Press.

An excellent book giving a detailed account of the research process but the material is not always related to early years contexts.

# Conclusion

This book has been written for students of Early Childhood Studies. The content is aimed at developing an awareness of how social science can be applied to Early Childhood Studies. Subjects in the social sciences provide a number of potential explanations for complex aspects of human behaviour. This is one of the reasons why subjects such as psychology, sociology and social policy are such an integral part of the Early Childhood Studies academic syllabus. Each of the main chapters has included formative activities in order to raise awareness of the significance of social science for Early Childhood Studies.

## Book structure

The book has adopted an interactive approach by using reflective activities and case studies in each of the main chapters. This is to ensure that the main learning themes are applied to specific concerns in early years. Each of the chapters has attempted to engage the reader with issues that are of importance to early years. It is hoped that this book is more than a general social science textbook because the content places social science within the everyday context of early years practice.

# Chapter themes

The book's chapters have concentrated upon particular aspects of social science in relation to Early Childhood Studies. Chapter 1 applies psychology to the early years context. The differing schools of psychological thought have been considered alongside working with children and families. Whereas behaviourist psychologists such as Skinner have emphasized the importance of external environmental factors in producing thoughts, humanists such as Rogers have placed an emphasis upon the importance of unique individuals processing thoughts that have been generated by the environment in a highly original way. The chapter outlines the importance of adopting as holistic an approach to psychology as possible if the subject is to be applied to early years. The therapies that are offered to early years from each perspective of psychology have merits that depend upon the particular context within which the therapies are being applied. Moreover, this holistic approach to applying psychological therapies to early years appears to support collaborative provision and interagency working. This is an important policy theme within the children's workforce in general.

Chapter 2 has explored the application of sociology to Early Childhood Studies. The ideas within sociological perspectives such as functionalism, interactionism and conflict theory have been considered in developing the argument that social factors are particularly important for children's growth and development. The application of sociology to early years has been considered through exemplification and critical appraisal of sociological perspectives in relation to Early Childhood Studies.

Chapter 3 has discussed the importance of social policy for Early Childhood Studies. The chapter has explained what social policy is, alongside analysing how social policy impacts upon the work of the children's workforce. The chapter also offers a critical appraisal of the implications of selected social policies for early years. It is essential to become aware of the key social policy legislation that shapes the early years context. A key theme is the emphasis that is placed on partnership and integrated working. There has occurred the emergence of a policy ideal that the children's workforce ought to be characterized by different sectors working together in order to find what has been referred to as 'joined-up solutions to joined-up problems'. The chapter also explored the idea that the emphasis being placed on 'partnership' and 'working together' assumes that this model of practice is possible. The deep-seated social divisions that can characterize UK society may mean that a model of partnership and working collaboration becomes more of an 'ideal' than a 'reality'. The effectiveness of current government policy directions can be considered in view of this.

Chapters 4 and 5 explore some of the issues that are associated with pedagogy, enhancing learning and Early Childhood Studies. The chapters focus on how children's learning and practitioner teaching develops with experience. A main theme of the chapters is exploring how the child's personality, thought processes and capacity for learning develop over time. It is important for teachers in early years to place children's development within context. The chapter reveals that there are a number of differing ways of understanding pedagogy. A number of important experiences appear to influence the child's ability to learn. The chapter reveals that it is important to adopt the holistic approach to child development that was recommended in Chapter 1. In other words, as opposed to regarding children's learning as being influenced by either 'biology' or 'social factors', it is important to accept that there are a combination of psychosocial and biological factors that appear to influence children's development. As opposed to adopting an 'either/or' approach to pedagogy we need to adopt as broad a perspective as possible.

The final chapter has discussed research methods for Early Childhood Studies. After identifying what the terms 'research' means, the chapter explores ways that the research process can be applied to early years. The chapter identifies the different research models and methods that are available to students studying Early Childhood Studies. The content of the chapter also considers the importance of having a manageable research focus. Research is one of the most important aspects of academic work within Early Childhood Studies. We need to conduct research into professional practice in order to identify how the profession can move forward. The design of our research question and its associated methodology become critical to the process of identifying what needs to be changed within the children's workforce.

The book aims to make a contribution to enhancing the professional development of the children's workforce. If this occurs it will achieve the highest of aims. There cannot be a more important professional role than helping children to develop. After all, today's children are tomorrow's adults and they represent the social future for generations to come.

# Answers

## Chapter 1: Psychology and Early Childhood Studies (pp. 5–29)

### Answer 1

The five major schools of psychology are: psychoanalytical, behaviourist, humanistic, neurobiological and cognitive.

### Answer 2

The best way of applying psychology to early years is through holistic therapies that combine the principles of behaviourism, humanism, cognitive, psychodynamic and neurobiological psychology to meeting the complex needs of individuals.

### Answer 3

| School of thought | Strength | Weakness |
|---|---|---|
| Behaviourism | Acknowledgement of environmental influences on the mind. | A tendency to neglect individual creativity with external factors. |
| Humanism | Acknowledgement of how individuals manipulate external variables. | Rogerian theory is idealistic. |
| Psychodynamic | Acknowledgement of the workings of the unconscious mind. | The theory is not methodologically proven. |
| Cognitive | Acknowledgement of the different thought processes during human cognitive development. | The idea of stages of development is not necessarily the case. Cognitive development is more a process than a series of stages. |
| Neurobiological | Acknowledgement of the link between human thoughts and hormones/chromosomes. | The theory is biologically reductionist. |

# Chapter 2: Sociology and Early Childhood Studies (pp. 31–52)

### Answer 1
Three influential sociological perspectives are functionalism, interactionism and conflict theory.

### Answer 2
The best way of applying sociology to early years is through combining the perspectives with psychological therapies in order to meet the complex needs of children and families.

### Answer 3

| School of thought | Strength | Weakness |
|---|---|---|
| Functionalism | Acknowledgement of the importance of the social system. | A tendency to neglect individuals who negotiate social meanings. |
| Interactionism | Acknowledgement of the importance of creative individuals generating social meanings. | A tendency to focus on the role of individuals to the detriment of wider social structures. |
| Conflict theory | Acknowledgement of the importance of economics. | A tendency to reduce social factors to economic variables. |

### Answer 4
The teaching arrangements for children today are different to how they were in the past. This view is expressed by a former headmaster who asked a parent what their son had done on his first day in school. The parent explained that the little boy had gone into the classroom and sat on the carpet with all the rest of the children. The retired headmaster found it difficult to understand how this had happened. 'Was Michael not led into the classroom, shown to his desk and made to listen to the teacher?' asked the headmaster. This reveals how educational practice changes over time. Social processes are not uniform. They vary through the years. The advantage of Foucault's work is that it draws attention to how and why institutions change. Some of Foucault's most celebrated work investigates how the treatment of the mentally ill has changed over time in countries like the United Kingdom. Whereas the mentally ill used to be incarcerated in prison-like institutions, they are now cared for in smaller caring homes. Whereas the mentally ill were once removed

from society, they are now integrated into society. This change has resulted from a complex set of political, economic, medical and social circumstances. Foucault explores how individuals and social institutions combine together to produce this change. His work suggests that understandings of teaching and learning in early years will continue to change over time. We could argue that perhaps Foucault's emphasis on political, economic, institutional and social factors means that the creative impact of individuals is overlooked. There is also possibly less credit given to the ways that individuals can resist power as opposed to being formed by power. Nonetheless, Foucault's work reveals that societies like the United Kingdom are a complex combination of factors resulting in exciting variations of social relations. This in turn sounds like the definition of sociology that we used at the beginning of Chapter 2!

# Chapter 3: Social Policy and Early Childhood Studies (pp. 53–78)

### Answer 1
New Labour and the coalition's key policy theme is 'partnership'.

### Answer 2
Four areas of recent examples of government policy affecting early years are Every Child Matters, mentoring, multiple intelligences and ICTs.

### Answer 3
A strength of New Labour is the importance that is given to statutory services. A weakness of the emphasis on partnership is that it is difficult to be 'all things to all people'. To apply the familiar saying, it is impossible to please all of the people all of the time!

# Chapter 4: Pedagogy and Early Childhood Studies (pp. 80–109)

1. Learning is a relatively permanent change in behaviour.
2. Advertising works by association. This means that a stimulus is associated with a positive response.
3. This varies according to the individual (e.g. when I teach my lessons well, my programme leader gives me a lovely Christmas card!).
4. Behaviourists believe that behaviour is based on learning.

5.  A major cognitive theorist is Piaget.
6.  Carl Rogers, Abraham Maslow and Malcolm Knowles.
7.  Surface learning can be described as shallow or superficial as it is simply the recalling of factual information.
8.  Teaching by asking (instead of teaching by telling), ask higher-order questions (Bloom's taxonomy), use case studies.

# Chapter 5: Enhancing learning and Early Childhood Studies (pp. 112–32)

**Answer 1**

Inclusive practice is the use of a variety of differentiated approaches to teaching in the classroom. This is in order to deliver the curriculum in a way that promotes access to learning for as many learners as possible.

**Answer 2**

- Course content and overall aims of the course.
- Time constraints.
- The content of the curriculum to be delivered and the appropriate order of delivery.
- The teaching and learning strategies and the type of knowledge and skills to be developed.
- Any requirements of national curriculum standards.
- Assessment of learning.
- Specialist knowledge input.
- The available physical and human resources.
- Specific detail about children's entry behaviour and the individual learning needs of each child.
- Learning styles.
- Abilities of the learners.
- Equality and diversity issues.

**Answer 3**

Brookfield's 'lenses' include:

- our own perspective;
- the point of view of our learners;
- the point of view of our colleagues;
- reflection on pedagogical theory.

# Chapter 6: Research methods and Early Childhood Studies (pp. 134–62)

**Answer 1**

The three research models that are especially relevant to early years are the positivist, interpretive and action research perspectives.

**Answer 2**

The best way of applying the research process to early years is through identifying a possible topic of 'action research' so that the research can be used to inform future professional practice.

**Answer 3**

| Research model | Strength | Weakness |
| --- | --- | --- |
| Positivist | Acknowledgement of quantitative data. | A tendency to neglect individuals creating social meaning. |
| Interpretive | Acknowledgement of how individuals negotiate meaning. | Research is usually small-scale and localized. |
| Action research | The research can be used to inform future professional practice. | It is difficult to be 'impartial' as an action researcher as you are intimately involved with the research process. |

# References

## Introduction

Clark, M. and Waller, T. (2007), *Early Childhood Education and Care: Policy and Practice*. London: Sage.

Doyle, C. (2005), 'Protecting children', in T. Waller (ed.), *Early Childhood: A Multidisciplinary Approach*. London: Paul Chapman (pp. 96–110).

Handley, G. (2005), 'Children's rights to participation', in T. Waller (ed.), *An Introduction To Early Childhood: A Multidisciplinary Approach*. London: Paul Chapman (pp. 1–12).

McGillivray, G. (2007), 'Policy and practice in England', in M. Clark and T. Waller (eds), *Early Childhood Education and Care: Policy and Practice*. London: Sage (pp. 20–50).

## Chapter 1

Audi, R. (1995), *The Cambridge Dictionary of Philosophy*. Cambridge: Cambridge University Press.

Diamond, M. (1980), *Sexual Decisions*. London: Little Brown.

Gorski, R., McLean-Evans, H. and Whalen, R. (1966), *The Brain and Gonadal Function*. CA: University of California Press.

Gross, R. D. (2001), *Psychology: The Science of Mind and Behaviour*. London: Hodder Arnold.

Kesey, K. (1962), *One Flew Over the Cuckoo's Nest*. London: Picador.

Kohler, W. (1927), *The Mentality of Apes*. London: Kegan Paul.

Malim, T. and Birch, A. (1998), *Introductory Psychology*. London: Palgrave Macmillan.

Online Dictionary (online at: www.dictionary.reference.com).

Watson, A. (2004), 'Reconfiguring the public sphere: implications for analyses of educational policy', *British Journal of Educational Studies*, 52(2), 228–48.

## Chapter 2

Allbrow, M. (1970), *Bureaucracy*. London: Macmillan.

Audi, R. (1995), *The Cambridge Dictionary of Philosophy*. Cambridge: Cambridge University Press.

Berger, P. (1966), *Invitation to Sociology*. London: Hamondsworth.

Bourdieu, P. (1986), *Questions de sociologie*. Paris: Les Editions de Minuit.

— (1992), *Language and Symbolic Power*. Cambridge: Polity Press.

— (1993), *Outline of a Theory of Practice*. Cambridge: Cambridge University Press.

Davis, K. (1948), *Human Society*. New York: Macmillan.

Durkheim, E. (1984/1893), *The Division of Labour in Society*. Basingstoke: Macmillan.

— (1899), 'Two laws of penal evolution', *L'année sociologique*, IV, 65–95.

— (1952), *Suicide: A Study in Sociology*. London: Routledge Kegan & Paul.

— (2002), *Moral Education*. New York: Dover publications.

Foucault, M. (1971), *Madness and Civilisation*. London: Routledge.

— (1977), *Discipline and Punish*. London: Allen Lane.

Gardner, H. (1985), *Frames of Mind: The Theory of Multiple Intelligence*. New York: Basic Books.

*Guardian Online*, 15 October 2011 (online at: www.guardian.co.uk).

Habermas, J. (1981), *The Theory of Communicative Action*. London: Heinemann.

House of Commons Work and Pensions Committee, 15 July 2011 (online at: www.publications.parliament.uk).

Hudson, B. (2003), *Understanding Justice: An Introduction to Ideas, Perspectives and Controversies in Modern Penal History*. Buckinghamshire: Open University Press.

Lipsett, A. (2007), 'Darling announces extra education spend' (online at: www.education.guardian.co.uk).

Lopez, J. and Scott, J. (2000), *Social Structure*. Buckingham: Open University Press.

Marshall, G. (1994), *Oxford Dictionary of Sociology*. Oxford: Oxford University Press.

McLellan, D. (1986), *Marx*. London: Fontana.

McNay, L. (1994), *Foucault: A Critical Introduction*. Cambridge: Polity Press.

Mills, C. W. (1959), *The Sociological Imagination*. Oxford: Oxford University Press.

Online Dictionary, 15 July 2011 (online at: www.dictionary.reference.com).

Orwell, G. (1949), *Nineteen Eighty-Four*. London: Penguin Books Ltd.

Parton, N. (2005), *Safeguarding children: early intervention and surveillance in late modern society*. London: Palgrave Macmillan.

Taylor, P., Richardson, J., Yeo, A., Marsh, I., Trobe, K. and Pilkington, A. (2004), *Sociology in Focus*. Ormskirk: Causeway Press.

Weber, M. (1968), *Economy and Society: An Outline of Interpretive Sociology*. New York: Bedminster Press.

Whitehead, P. (2010), 'Social theory and probation: exploring organisational complexity within a modernising context', *Social and Public Policy Review*, 4(4), 15–33.

Zedner, L. (2004), *Criminal Justice*. Oxford: Oxford University Press.

# Chapter 3

Alcock, C., Payne, S. and Sullivan, M. (2000), *Introducing Social Policy*. Harlow: Prentice Hall.

Bers, M. (2008), *Blocks to Robots: Learning with Technology in the Early Childhood Classroom*. New York: Teachers College Press.

— (2010), 'Virtual worlds as playgrounds for learning', paper presented at the *International Virtual Environments Research Group Conference*, 28–29 June 2010, Teesside University, UK.

Binfield, M. (2006), 'Lack of duty acts as barrier to social care support for homeless people', 2 February 2006 (online at: www.communitycare.co.uk).

Blakemore, K. (2003), *Social Policy: An Introduction*. Buckingham: Open University Press.

Brookes, W. (2005), 'The graduate teacher programme in England: mentor training, quality assurance and the findings of inspection', *Journal of In-Service Education*, 31(1), 43–61.

Clegg, S., Hudson, A. and Steel, J. (2010), 'The emperor's new clothes: globalisation and e-learning in Higher Education', *British Journal of Sociology of Education*, 24(1), 39–53.

Coffield, F. (1999), 'Breaking the consensus: lifelong learning as social control', *British Educational Research Journal*, 25(4), 479–99.

— (2004), *Should We be Using Learning Styles?* London: Learning and Skills Research Centre.

Cook, D. (2004), ICT and curriculum provision in the early years. In: Miller, L. and Deveraux, J. (2004), *Supporting Children's Learning in the Early Years*. Abingdon: David Fulton Publishers (pp. 154–164).

DFES (2006), 'Evaluating the EYSEFD: a qualitative experience of employers' and mentors' experiences', *Research Report 752*. London: Stationery Office.

Dicey, A. (1962), *Lectures on the Relation between Law and Public Opinion in England During the Nineteenth Century*. London: Palgrave Macmillan.

Drotner, K., Siggard Jensen, H. and Christian Schroeder, K. (2008), *Informal Learning and Digital Media*. Newcastle: Cambridge Scholars Publishing.

Gardner, H. (1984), *Frames of Mind: The Theory of Multiple Intelligence*. New York: Basic Books.

— (1993), *Multiple Intelligences: The Theory in Practice*. New York: Basic Books Limited.

— (2000), *Intelligence Reframed: Multiple Intelligences for the 21st Century*. New York: Basic Books.

Giddens, A. (2004), *The Third Way and its Critics*. Cambridge: Polity Press.

Harris, B. (2004), *The Origins of the British Welfare State*. Basingstoke: Palgrave Macmillan.

Ingleby, E. (2010), 'Robbing Peter to pay Paul: the price of standards-driven education', *Research in Post-Compulsory Education*, 15(1), 427–41.

— (2011), 'Asclepius or Hippocrates? Differing interpretations of post-compulsory initial teacher training mentoring', *Journal of Vocational Education & Training*, 63(1), 15–25.

Ingleby, E. and Hunt, J. (2008), 'The cpd needs of mentors in initial teacher training in England', *Journal of In-Service Education*, 34(1), 61–74.

Kesey, K. (1962), *One Flew Over the Cuckoo's Nest*. London: Picador.

Law, C. (1967), 'The growth of urban population in England and Wales, 1801–1911', *Transactions of the Institute of British Geographers*, 41(1), 125–43.

Lucas, N. (2007), 'The in-service training of adult literacy, numeracy, and English for speakers of other languages: the challenges of a "standards led model"', *Journal of In-Service Education*, 33(1), 125–42.

Lumsden, E. (2005), 'Joined up thinking in practice: an exploration of professional collaboration', in T. Waller (ed.), *An Introduction to Early Childhood: A Multidisciplinary Approach*. London: Paul Chapman (pp. 152–166).

Marsh, J., Brooks, G., Hughes, J., Ritchie, L., Roberts, S. and Wright, K. (2005), *Digital Beginnings: Young People's Use of Popular Culture, New Media and New Technologies*. Sheffield: University of Sheffield.

Malderez, A. (2001), 'New ELT professionals', *English Teaching Professional*, 19(1), 57–8.

Moore, S. (2002), *Social Welfare Alive*. Cheltenham: Nelson Thornes.

Plath, S. (1963), *The Bell Jar*. London: Faber and Faber.

Plowman, L. and Stephen, C. (2005), 'Children, play and computers in pre-school education', *British Journal of Educational Technology*, 36(2), 145–57.

Scull, A. (1982), *Museums of Madness: The Social Organisation of Insanity in Nineteenth-Century England*. Harmondsworth: Penguin.

Schuller, T. and Burns, A. (1999), 'Using social capital to compare performance in continuing education', in F. Coffield (ed.), *Why's the Beer Always Stronger up North? Studies in Lifelong Learning in Europe*. Bristol: Polity Press (pp. 53–61).

Tedder, M. and Lawy, R. (2009), 'The pursuit of "excellence": mentoring in further education initial teacher training in England', *Journal of Vocational Education and Training*, 61(4), 413–29.

Watson, A. (2004), 'Reconfiguring the public sphere: implications for analyses of educational policy', *British Journal of Educational Studies*, 52(3), 228–48.

Winter, J. (1986), *The Great War and the British People*. Basingstoke: Palgrave Macmillan.

Yelland, N. and Kilderry, A. (2010), 'Becoming numerate with information technologies in the twenty-first century', *International Journal of Early Years Education*, 18(2), 91–106.

# Chapter 4

Atherton, J. S. (2009), 'Learning and teaching; cognitive theories of learning', 21 December 2011 (online at: www.learningandteaching.info/learning/cognitive.htm).

Atkinson, R. L., Atkinson, R. C., Smith, E. E. and Bem, D. J. (1993), *Introduction to Psychology* (11th edn). Fort Worth, TX: Harcourt Brace Jovanovich.

Bloom, B. S. (1956), *Taxonomy of Educational Objectives, the Classification of Educational Goals – Handbook I: Cognitive Domain*. New York: McKay.

Haughton, E. (2004), 'Learning and teaching theory', 21 December 2011 (online at: www.learning-theories.com).

Knowles, M. S. (1950), *Informal Adult Education*. Chicago: Association Press.

Marton, F. and Saljo, R. (1984), 'On qualitative differences in learning. Outcomes as a function of the learner's conception of the task', *British Journal of Educational Psychology*, 46(1), 115–27.

Maslow, A. (1987), *Motivation and Personality* (3rd edn). New York: Harper and Row.

Petty, G. (2009), *Teaching Today* (4th edn). Cheltenham: Nelson Thornes.

Rogers, C. (1983), *Freedom to Learn*. New York. Merrill.

Tulving, E. (1985), 'How many memory systems are there?', *American Psychologist*, 40(1), 385–98.

Skinner, B. F. (1953), *Science and Human Behaviour*. New York: Macmillan.

# Chapter 5

Brookfield, S. (1985), *Becoming a Critically Reflective Teacher*. San Francisco, CA: Jossey-Bass.

Brown, S., Armstrong, A. and Thompson, G. (1998), *Motivating Students*. Birmingham: SEDA Publications.

Coffield, F. (2004), *Learning Styles*. London: LSDA Publications.

Fry, H., Ketteridge, S. and Marshall, S. (2003), *A Handbook for Teaching and Learning in Higher Education* (2nd edn). London: Routledge Falmer.

Gardner, H. (1993), *Frames of Mind: The Theory of Multiple Intelligences* (2nd edn). London: Fontana Press.

Gravells, A. and Simpson, S. (2009), *Equality and Diversity in the Lifelong Learning Sector*. Exeter: Learning Matters.

Kelly, A. V. (2004), *The Curriculum, Theory and Practice* (5th edn). London: Sage.

Lave, J. and Wenger, E. (1990), *Situated Learning: Legitimate Peripheral Participation*. Cambridge: Cambridge University Press.

Petty, G. (2009), *Teaching Today* (4th edn). Cheltenham: Nelson Thornes.

Tennant, M. (1997), *Psychology and Adult Education* (2nd edn). Oxfordshire: Routledge.

Tomlinson, C. A. (1997), *Differentiation of Instruction in Mixed Ability Classrooms*. Idaho: Idaho Council for Exceptional Children.

— (2001), *How to Differentiate Instruction in Mixed Ability Classrooms* (2nd edn). Alexandria: Association for Supervision and Curriculum Development.

Tummons, J. (2009), *Curriculum Studies in the Lifelong Learning Sector*. Exeter: Learning Matters.

Vygotsky, L. S. (1978), *Mind in Society, the Development of Higher Psychological Processes*. Cambridge, MA: Harvard University Press.

## Chapter 6

Audi, R. (1995), *The Cambridge Dictionary of Philosophy*. Cambridge: Cambridge University Press.

Brookes, W. (2005), 'The graduate teacher training programme in England: mentor training quality assurance and the findings of inspection', *Journal of In-Service Education*, 31(1), 43–61.

Bryman, A. (2004), *Social Research Methods*. Oxford: Oxford University Press.

Bryman, A. and Cramer, D. (1997), *Quantitative Data Analysis: A Guide for Social Scientists*. London: Routledge.

Chambers, R. (1983), *Rural Development: Putting the Last First*. London: Longman.

Denzin, N. K. and Lincoln, Y. (2000), *The Handbook of Qualitative Research*. Thousand Oaks, CA: Sage.

Freire, P. (1970), *Pedagogy of the Oppressed*. London: Continuum.

Gillham, B. (2000), *Case Study Research Methods*. London: Continuum.

Geertz, C. (1973), *The Interpretation of Cultures: Selected Essays*. New York: Basic Books.

— (1988), *Works and Lives: The Anthropologist as Author*. Stanford, CA: Stanford University Press.

— (1993), *Local Knowledge: Further Essays in Interpretive Anthropology*. London: Fontana Press.

Green, S. and Hogan, D. (2005), *Researching Children's Experience: Approaches and Methods*. London: Sage Publications.

Hale, J. A. (2008), *A Guide to Curriculum Planning*. Thousand Oaks, CA: Corwin Press.

House of Commons Work and Pensions Committee, 15 November 2011 (online at: www.publications. parliament.uk).

Ingleby, E. (2010), 'Robbing Peter to pay Paul: the price of standards-driven education', *Research in Post-Compulsory Education*, 15(1), 427–40.

Ingleby, E. and Hunt, J. (2008), 'The CPD needs of mentors in post-compulsory Initial Teacher Training in England', *Journal of In-Service Education*, 34(1), 61–75.

Kreuger, R. (1994), *Moderating Focus Groups*. Thousand Oaks, CA: Sage.

Lucas, N. (2007), 'The in-service training of adult literacy, numeracy and English for speakers of other languages teachers in England; the challenges of a 'standards-led model', *Journal of In-Service Education*, 33(1), 125–42.

Munday, J. (2006), 'Identity in focus: the use of focus groups to study the construction of collective identity', *Sociology*, 40(1), 89–105.

Online Dictionary, 15 November 2011 (online at: www.dictionary.reference.com).

Opie, C. (2004), *Doing Educational Research: A Guide to First Time Researchers*. London: Sage.

Parker-Rees, R., Leeson, C., Willan, J. and Savage, J. (2004), *Early Childhood Studies*. Exeter: Learning Matters.

Simpson, D. (2010), 'Becoming professional? Exploring early years professional status and its implications for workforce reform in England', *Journal of Early Childhood Research*, 8(1), 269–81.

# Index